CYCLING THE RUTA
VÍA DE LA PLATA

CYCLING THE RUTA VÍA DE LA PLATA

ON AND OFF-ROAD OPTIONS ON THE CAMINO FROM SEVILLE TO SANTIAGO AND GIJÓN

by John Hayes

JUNIPER HOUSE, MURLEY MOSS,
OXENHOLME ROAD, KENDAL, CUMBRIA LA9 7RL
www.cicerone.co.uk

© John Hayes 2022
First edition 2022
ISBN: 978 1 78631 012 5

Printed in India by Replika Press Pvt. Ltd using responsibly sourced paper.
A catalogue record for this book is available from the British Library.
All photographs are by the author unless otherwise stated.

Route mapping by Lovell Johns www.lovelljohns.com
Contains OpenStreetMap.org data © OpenStreetMap
contributors, CC-BY-SA. NASA relief data courtesy of ESRI

Acknowledgements

Many thanks to the staff at the Ruta Vía de la Plata Association who organised
my trip in 2019. I'm especially grateful for the tours they set up in each of the
major towns on the Ruta, providing invaluable local input into my research.

Updates to this Guide

While every effort is made by our authors to ensure the accuracy of
guidebooks as they go to print, changes can occur during the lifetime of an
edition. Any updates that we know of for this guide will be on the Cicerone
website (www.cicerone.co.uk/1012/updates), so please check before
planning your trip. We also advise that you check information about such
things as transport, accommodation and shops locally. Even rights of way
can be altered over time.

We are always grateful for information about any discrepancies
between a guidebook and the facts on the ground, sent by email to
updates@cicerone.co.uk or by post to Cicerone, Juniper House, Murley
Moss, Oxenholme Road, Kendal, LA9 7RL.

Register your book: To sign up to receive free updates, special offers
and GPX files where available, register your book at www.cicerone.co.uk.

Front cover: Enjoying the Ruta Vía de la Plata on and off-road

CONTENTS

Route summary tables 8

INTRODUCTION 11
The route 12
The cycling. 14
A ride through Spain's history 15
Landscape 19
Climate and when to go 20
Wildlife 21
Choosing your route 22
Accommodation. 22
Food. 24
Getting there 25
What to take. 28
Navigation 29
Using this guide 30

RUTA VÍA DE LA PLATA. 33
Stage 1   Seville to El Real de la Jara 34
Stage 2   El Real de la Jara to Zafra 46
Stage 3   Zafra to Mérida 54
Stage 4   Mérida to Cáceres. 63
Stage 5   Cáceres to Grimaldo 74
Stage 6   Grimaldo to Plasencia. 82
Stage 7   Plasencia to Béjar 89
Stage 8   Béjar to Salamanca 100
Stage 9   Salamanca to Zamora 110
Stage 10   Zamora to Benavente 119
Stage 11   Benavente to León. 127
Stage 12   León to Pola de Lena. 139
Stage 13   Pola de Lena to Oviedo. 150
Stage 14   Oviedo to Gijón 156

CAMINO SANABRÉS 163
Stage 1S   Zamora to Tábara 164
Stage 2S   Tábara to Puebla de Sanabria 171
Stage 3S   Puebla de Sanabria to A Gudiña 180
Stage 4S   A Gudiña to Ourense 187
Stage 5S   Ourense to Lalín 197
Stage 6S   Lalín to Santiago de Compostela 205

Appendix A   Accommodation 214
Appendix B   Useful contacts 217
Appendix C   Glossary 218

Note on Mapping

The route maps in this guide are derived from publicly available data, databases and crowd-sourced data. As such they have not been through the detailed checking procedures that would generally be applied to a published map from an official mapping agency. However, we have reviewed them closely in the light of local knowledge as part of the preparation of this guide.

ROUTE SUMMARY TABLES

Stage	RUTA VÍA DE LA PLATA							Page
	Road		Off-road		Hybrid/recommended			
	Distance	Time	Distance	Time	Distance	Time		
Stage 1 – Seville to El Real de la Jara	87km	4hr 50min	82km	7hr	80km	5hr 30min		34
Stage 2 – El Real de la Jara to Zafra	90km	4hr 55min	77km	6hr	77km	5hr 40min		46
Stage 3 – Zafra to Mérida	63km	3hr 45min	63km	4hr 50min	63km (same as off road route)	4hr 50min		54
Stage 4 – Mérida to Cáceres	69km	4hr 25min	78km	5hr 55min	78km	5hr 25min		63
Stage 5 – Cáceres to Grimaldo	52km	3hr 30min	53km	5hr 20min	52km	4hr 10min		74
Stage 6 – Grimaldo to Plasencia	33km	2hr	42km	3hr 40min	42km (same as off road route)	3hr 40min		82
Stage 7 – Plasencia to Béjar	57km	4hr 5min	79km	6hr 55min	74km*	6hr 10min		89
Stage 8 – Béjar to Salamanca	79km	5hr	81km	7hr	84km	6hr 50min		100
Stage 9 – Salamanca to Zamora	68km	3hr 35min	70km	5hr 40min	69km	4hr 40min		110
Stage 10 – Zamora to Benavente	66km	3hr 50min	68km	5hr	66km	4hr 15min		119
Stage 11 – Benavente to León	102km	6hr 5min	102km	7hr 20min	102km (same as off-road route)	7hr 20min		127
Stage 12 – León to Pola de Lena	84km	5hr	95km	8hr 30min	94km	7hr 30min		139
Stage 13 – Pola de Lena to Oviedo	36km	2hr 30min	37km	3hr 30min	36km (same as road route)	3hr 30min		150

RUTA VÍA DE LA PLATA

Stage	Road		Off-road		Hybrid/recommended		Page
	Distance	Time	Distance	Time	Distance	Time	
Stage 14 – Oviedo to Gijón	44km	3hr 15min	36km	3hr 40min	36km (same as off-road route)	3hr 40min	156
Total	**930km**	**56hr 45min**	**963km**	**80hr 20min**	**957km**	**72hr 20min**	

* add 10km and 45min for Hervás

CAMINO SANABRÉS

Stage	Road		Off-road		Hybrid		Page
	Distance	Time	Distance	Time	Distance	Time	
Stage 1S – Zamora to Tábara	61km	4hr 20min	68km	5hr 20min	62km	4hr 45min	164
Stage 2S – Tábara to Puebla de Sanabria	86km	4hr 55min	97km	7hr 45min	95km	7hr 10min	171
Stage 3S – Puebla de Sanabria to A Gudiña	59km	3hr 55min	53km	4hr 55min	59km	4hr	180
Stage 4S – A Gudiña to Ourense	97km	5hr 45min	89km	7hr 20min	90km	6hr 40min	187
Stage 5S – Ourense to Lalín	51km	3hr 20min	57km	4hr 45min	57km (same as off-road route)	4hr 45min	197
Stage 6S – Lalín to Santiago de Compostela	50km	3hr 15min	55km	4hr 50min	55km (same as off-road route)	4hr 50min	205
Total (including all stages from Seville)	**1002km**	**61hr 35min**	**1044km**	**87hr 15min**	**1040km**	**78hr 10min**	

Ready for departure on the Ruta Vía de la Plata (Stage 1)

INTRODUCTION

An alternative way to travel (Stage 4)

Cycling the Ruta Vía de la Plata (RVP) takes you through the heart of Spain from south to north. It's a celebrated two-week journey that visits amazing towns and cities, crosses huge and varied landscapes and brings to life Spain's rich culture and fascinating history.

The Ruta was a trading route long before the Romans arrived but it was the Romans who put real infrastructure in place. Their route, with its paved surface ('la Plata'), ran from Mérida in southern Spain (the capital of the Roman province of Lusitana), north across the Spanish plateau through to Astorga at the foot of the Cantabrian mountains. The Visigoths and the Muslims continued to use it, but as the Christians drove south in the 12th and 13th centuries it took on a new purpose – that of a pilgrimage route taking travellers from Seville up to Santiago de Compostela. The ever-expanding Castilian kingdom gained further momentum with the 'discovery' of the Americas, when gold and silver flooded into Spain, via Seville, and north to the towns and cities along the RVP.

The Ruta contributed directly to the wealth and prosperity of its towns and cities, providing a fabulous legacy for today's traveller. Seville, Mérida, Plasencia, Cáceres, Salamanca, Zamora, León and Santiago de Compostela – with their UNESCO World Heritage status – would justify a trip to Spain in their own right.

The RVP is well-known in Spain. The 'brand' is extensively used and to some degree has been stretched and bent. For those promoting the pilgrimage, the route starts in Seville and finishes in Santiago de Compostela. Others, who focus on its Roman origins and function as a trading route, insist it goes over the Cantabrian mountains and on to Gijón on the north coast. Each route has its pros and cons, and this guidebook provides the information needed to make a choice between them.

Spain is a superb country for cycling. The weather is good, the food and drink excellent and accommodation is great value. Although Spanish cycling is not as organised as in northern Europe – designated long-distance cycleways are only just beginning to feature – the roads are comparatively empty and there is huge scope for non-challenging off-road cycling.

The RVP works for a broad spectrum of cyclists, with both road and off-road routes. Furthermore, there are frequent intersections, meaning a touring cyclist can get the best of both worlds.

This guidebook assumes a journey of 14 days along the Ruta Vía de la Plata to Gijón, and 15 days if the pilgrimage route along the Camino Sanabrés to Santiago de Compostela is followed. The first nine days are the same for both journeys, with the option along the Santiago de Compostela route turning west at Granja de Moreruela just north of Zamora on Day 10. Completing the route in 14 or 15 days is a realistic timetable for a reasonably fit touring cyclist willing to sample the agricultural trails typical of the off-road route; and a very generous schedule for the road cyclist, who could complete both routes with three days to spare.

This guidebook has been developed with the support of the Ruta Vía de la Plata Association. The association consists of representatives from towns and cities along the route, from Seville to Gijón, who work together to promote its tourist potential for walkers, cyclists, motorcyclists and motorists. It maintains a wonderful website packed with useful information, and the association's help in the development of this guidebook has been invaluable.

THE ROUTE

Although the original Roman road that established the RVP predates its use as a pilgrim route, it is now part of the growing network of Caminos. Starting in Seville it goes north through Andalucía, climbing gently out of the coastal plain. At El Real de la Jara, in the Parque Natural de

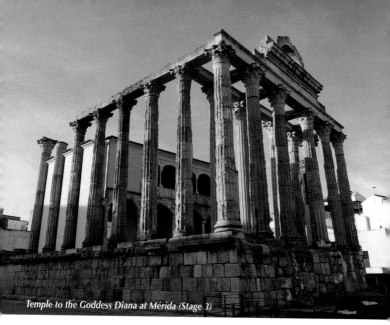

Temple to the Goddess Diana at Mérida (Stage 3)

la Jara, it crosses the Sierra Morena and the watershed between the Guadalquivir and the Guadiana rivers and climbs onto the *meseta* (Spain's central plateau). At the same time it leaves the region of Andalucía and heads into the Extremadura. After visiting Zafra it continues north to Mérida, the region's capital, where it is joined by the Camino Mozárabe, which has come up from Granada and Córdoba. North of Mérida, the route crosses another watershed (the westerly remnants of the Montes de Toledo), descends gently into the wide Río Tejo valley and continues, via Cáceres and Plasencia, to the border with Castilla y León. Here it crosses the Sierra de Gredos, north of which

rivers flow into the Duoro. From the watershed the route descends gently to Salamanca and Zamora (where it crosses the Duoro).

Just north of Zamora the route to Santiago de Compostela leaves the Ruta Vía de la Plata and joins the Camino Sanabrés. Heading west and initially following the Tera river, the route traverses three big passes before leaving Castilla y León and descending into Galicia. After visiting the city of Ourense, crossing its famous bridge, it finally arrives at Santiago de Compostela. The route passes through remote countryside, but because of the importance of the transport corridor, it is one that has had significant infrastructure investment. The construction of the motorway means that there is an empty N road (the N-525) for road cyclists and a fall-back for off-road cyclists whenever the Camino gets too tough or unpleasant.

Meanwhile, the Gijón route continues north on the RVP and visits Benavente. The original RVP continues to Astorga, but our Gijón route snips off a corner, misses out Astorga, and joins the Camino Francés (the main Santiago del Compostela pilgrimage route) travelling east into León against the flow of pilgrims (they are heading west). From León it joins the Camino del Salvador towards Oviedo, crossing from Castilla y León into Asturias at the watershed. From Oviedo it joins the Camino Primitivo to Gijón.

The off-road versions of the RVP and the Camino Sanabrés generally follow pilgrim routes and are way-marked with the yellow arrows typical in Spain. The road versions, for most of their duration, closely follow the N-630 (RVP) or the N-525 (Camino Sanabrés). The N-630 is also known as the Ruta Vía de la Plata. The N, or 'national' roads formed the first modern network and motorways often replicate their routes. In the case of the N-630, it has left a high-standard, wonderfully graded road used only by local traffic for road cyclists and a fall-back for off-road cyclists whenever the Camino gets too tough or unpleasant.

For those wanting a Spanish south–north 'coast to coast', this is easily put together and a recent extension to the Camino network, known as the Via Augusta and based on the old Roman road, now connects Seville with Cadiz in two days.

THE CYCLING

The RVP works well for a wide range of cyclists, from road cyclists through to mountain bikers. With good value food and accommodation, predictable weather, and plenty to see and experience at the end of each day, the RVP is an excellent cycle touring route. It's not particularly challenging – road cyclists looking for long ascents and mountain bikers seeking technical descents will be disappointed – but for most of those in between, it's a great choice. The road route intersects with the off-road at numerous points, providing a faster alternative or an escape for the off-road cyclist running low on fuel.

For road cyclists, the faster option is a particularly good route for a group, possibly a cycling club. Riders on fast road bikes don't generally carry gear, and a group with a back-up van would be able to complete the route a lot faster than the schedule proposed in this guidebook.

Touring cyclists can choose between the road and at least some off-road, much of which is based on farm tracks wide enough for agricultural vehicles. The route is well used by Spanish cyclists who typically favour mountain bikes with front

Early morning departure from Tabara (Stage 2 Camino Sanabrés)

suspension or a heavy-duty touring bike. Researching the off-road route for this guide, a 'gravel bike' (no suspension) fitted with wide tyres (40mm plus) on a 650b wheel was used. It coped well with 95 per cent of the off-road terrain and was much easier on-road than a mountain bike.

A RIDE THROUGH SPAIN'S HISTORY

Whichever route you choose there is a lot to see. The RVP follows a Roman road connecting towns and cities most of which were first settled more than 2000 years ago, and travelling along it is a journey through Spain's amazing history.

The Romans

The Romans first came to Iberia in 218BC to fight the Carthaginians for dominance of the western Mediterranean, but it wasn't until 19BC that Emperor Augustus was able to complete the conquest. After that it became one of the empire's most prized possessions and the birthplace of three emperors, including the hyperactive Hadrian. The imprint of Spain's Roman heritage is obvious (*la Plata* is the Arabic word for the Roman paving) and in places, on an often dead-straight route, original Roman mile markers still measure your progress.

Visigoths and Muslims

The Visigoths replaced the Romans in 472, but their impact is less obvious. The church became the most important institution and the tiny preRomanesque churches in the Asturias, among the oldest in Europe, are a Visigothic inheritance.

Easier to spot is the Muslim legacy. The Muslims arrived in Spain

in 711 and by 717 had crossed the Pyrenees into France. For 400 years Muslim Spain – *al Andalus* – was the most advanced part of western Europe, and its buildings, particularly fortifications, can be found all the way up the Ruta Vía de la Plata to León. León in fact was a northern outpost of Muslim-held Spain, essentially a fortress that protected its territory to the south until the 9th century. Seville has the most monumental Muslim legacy but other important buildings can be found in Mérida, Zamora and Cáceres.

A more profound legacy, and one which historians believe affects Spanish society even today, is the long struggle between Christians and Muslims for hegemony in the Iberian

peninsula and the ultimate triumph of the Christians, led by the Castilians.

Legend has it that the Battle of Covadonga in 722 marked the beginning of the Christian resurgence, but the Muslims held most of Spain until well into the 11th century. Different kingdoms in the north, sometimes in alliance with each other, sometimes in conflict and allied with the Muslims, conquered territory; but it wasn't until 1212, at the Battle of Las Navas de Tolosa, that the Christians achieved a decisive victory. Over the next 50 years, Muslim power in the peninsula was effectively ended, and although the Nasrid dynasty continued to rule in Granada until 1492, it was dominated by the growing power of Castile.

Reconquest

The process of reconquest has left its mark. Initially the process was slow, with peasants from the north repopulating the empty buffer zone in the Duoro valley while a limited number of relatively large towns were fortified to hold the territory. Some towns – Plasencia, for example – were built specifically for the purpose of territorial defence and both the towns and the peasantry enjoyed a degree of autonomy unusual in western Europe. After the Battle of Las Navas de Tolosa the pace of reconquest increased and became overtly religious, encouraged by Pope Urban II's call for a crusade. The process of repopulation became one of colonisation and the Muslims were evicted from the occupied territory. The recolonisers closest to the king were rewarded with huge land-holdings (*latifundia*). Spanish historians argue that the pace of the reconquest, faster in the south than the north, contributed to the relative underdevelopment of the south, and some even draw parallels with North and South America.

Arguably the size and distribution of towns along the RVP, with their heavily fortified medieval cores, and the relativity empty countryside between them, is a product of the reconquest. Because it was the Castilians who led this reconquest rather than the Aragonese (who, after conquering Valencia went on to build a Mediterranean empire) it was their language which came to dominate Spain.

The towns along the RVP were relatively successful even before the influx of wealth that came with the colonisation of the Americas. All of them had a Jewish quarter and the Jews were initially protected. From the 14th century onwards the mood changed and Jews became the subject of massacres and enforced conversion, a process policed by the newly established Spanish Inquisition. In 1492, Ferdinand and Isabel, whose marriage unified the crowns of Castile and Aragon and established the mainland borders of modern Spain, expelled the remaining 200,000 Jews, emptied all the Jewish quarters and initiated a migration whose descendants (Sephardic Jews) can now be found all over the world.

Monumental architecture

Spain's unique history plays out as you cycle through the countryside and visit the towns and cities. In particular the journey provides the opportunity to see some of the best examples of every important style of Spanish architecture and learn how they developed chronologically. Mérida, at the southern end of the Roman road and capital of the Roman province of Lusitania, has some of the most monumental examples of Roman architecture in Spain – in particular a huge amphitheatre and theatre, the world's longest Roman bridge, and an aqueduct. Ovieda, capital of the Asturias (the only part of Spain not occupied by the Muslims), has unique examples of pre-Romanesque architecture and some of the oldest churches in western Europe. Zamora, on the river Duoro, recaptured by the Christians relatively early, has the world's biggest concentration of Romanesque churches, while Romanesque churches and cathedrals feature in Seville, León, Cáceres and Plasencia.

As gold and silver flooded in from the Americas, towns and cities tried to outdo each other, and new cathedrals in the latest Gothic style were built in Salamanca, Plasencia and León only to be rendered old-fashioned by Renaissance buildings (with a distinct Spanish style known as plateresque) in Seville, Salamanca and León. The main square (Plaza Mayor) in Salamanca and the cathedral at Santiago de Compostela are regarded as masterpieces of Spanish Baroque architecture. To complete this architectural *tour de force* the route even includes important examples of Spanish modernisme, including, in León, one of only two Antoni Gaudi buildings outside Catalonia.

Repurposing

Although there are no Muslim masterpieces to compare with the Alhambra in Granada, Muslim architecture does feature, particularly in the fortifications (León, Zamora, Mérida, Cáceres), or was repurposed for subsequent use. For example the huge tower in the cathedral in Seville, La Giralda, was originally built by the Muslims as a minaret for the city's great mosque. Repurposing was common. The royal palace, the Alcázar, built near Seville's cathedral in the 14th century, used elements of a previous Muslim palace. This, in turn, was built using parts of an earlier Visigothic castle which, of course, owed its origins to Roman foundations. Moreover, the Alcázar is regarded as an important example of Mudéjar architecture where Islamic styles (often using Islamic craftsmen) are incorporated into Romanesque, Gothic and even Renaissance buildings.

The Barrio Húmedo in León

LANDSCAPE

The RVP's geography combines with historic patterns of land use to produce a unique and beautiful landscape – one that is best experienced on a bike.

After a short stretch on an intensively farmed flat coastal plain north of Seville, the Ruta climbs onto the main Spanish plateau (the *meseta*) which, apart from three gentle ridges, is fairly flat. It then continues gently over the Cantabrian mountains before descending precipitously down to the northern coastal strip which, unlike its cousin in the south, is not flat. If heading west, the Cantabrian mountains present a more significant barrier and three big passes have to be crossed before heading down into Galicia and Santiago de Compostela.

The landscape changes from south to north, but until you approach the north coast shares one defining characteristic – it's big and empty.

Compared to northern Europe, and the UK in particular, the population is confined to compact, tightly defined towns. This has something to do with climate and land productivity, but it's also a result of the process of repopulation and colonisation which accompanied the reconquest. The initial 100km-wide buffer zone between Christians and Muslims was in the Duoro valley and sheep farmers were the first people to exploit this relatively empty area. In the 12th century the buffer zone moved south into the Extremadura (wheat production moved into what was now a safer Duoro valley) and, with the introduction of merino sheep, Spain became hugely important as a wool producer.

The dehesa

A distinct feature of the first half the route is the *dehesa*. Best experienced off-road in May or June, when

19

the wild flowers are at their best, or in autumn when the grass has died off, it is a unique countryside and very beautiful. This is a fenced landscape organised in huge ranch-style farms (*latifundia*). Its defining feature is large-crowned evergreen oak trees (holm or cork oak) scattered, 30 or 40m apart, across huge open meadows. Only a few people make a living out such extensive livestock farming (originally sheep, but now a mix of cattle, sheep and the famous Spanish Ibérico black pigs) and forestry (cork, firewood and hunting). The trees, which seem to get darker as the year progresses and as the grass turns from green to yellow, cast intense shadows that protect the livestock from the summer sun. Riding through the *dehesa* is special, with the best day, on the stage from Placencia to Béjar, including an easy 40km stretch which approaches cycling bliss.

There is still a lot of *dehesa* left, although chunks of it were lost in the 1950s and 1960s when General Franco introduced land reform and a series of huge irrigation schemes. What might be the world's biggest vineyard, crossed on the approach to Mérida, is a product of this.

Another feature of the landscape, not so easy to spot but in its way just as impressive as the *dehesa*, are the Cañada Reales. These form a huge network of medieval livestock superhighways, established in the 13th century by royal edict, designed to get animals to and from the *dehesa* in the south twice a year, through the wheat fields, to the mountains in the north (transhumance). They were a regulation width (95 metres), wide enough to provide animals with enough fodder to keep them going in transit without damaging nearby crops. They were used until the late 20th century and some of them (particularly on the approach to Cáceres) follow the same route as the RVP.

The Cantabrians are a proper mountain range and after climbing into them the Mediterranean flora gives way to heather and something more north European. On the Gijón route in particular the towns and villages have an industrial heritage. There are different ways to traverse the mountains but it's worth remembering that the starting point is the plateau, so much of the climbing has already been done and the Gijón road route in particular involves only a gentle climb.

On the other side of the mountains there is an abrupt transformation, with Spain's Costa Verde ('Green Coast') extending along the north coast and around the corner into west-facing Galicia. Here the countryside feels busier with small dairy farms dominating the agricultural scene.

CLIMATE AND WHEN TO GO

Until the watershed is crossed in the Cantabrian mountains, the climate is a continental version of Mediterranean. The plateau, the *meseta*, can be cold and wet in the winter and very hot in the summer. Because of the altitude (between 500 and 800m), spring comes late on the *meseta* and, with heat just around the corner, is short. Climbing over the mountains, particularly on the Gijón route, the climate changes dramatically within the space of a few kilometres, with the continental climate replaced by moist, mild maritime conditions.

The best months for cycling the RVP are the second half of April, May and June, and September and October. July and August can be too hot, while winter on the Spanish plateau is often cold and wet. If there has been a lot of winter rain – and that seems to be a developing feature with climate change – parts of the route can be wet and streams that are normally minor obstacles may become problematic. Fortunately, even if the winter has been wet there is always the option of an empty road to fall back on.

WILDLIFE

The *dehesa* is one of Europe's most important bird habitats. Thumping along on a bike you'll be very lucky if you get to see a Spanish Imperial eagle, Eurasian black vulture, or Bonelli's eagle, but they can all be found in Extremadura. You'll be

| Month | Cáceres | | Oviedo | |
	Rainfall (mm)	Temp (av min/max C)	Rainfall (mm)	Temp (av min/max C)
Jan	60	3/11	80	6/15
Feb	40	4/12	80	6/15
March	20	6/17	80	7/15
April	60	9/19	100	8/16
May	40	10/21	90	9/18
June	30	15/29	60	14/22
July	10	19/33	40	15/23
Aug	10	19/32	60	15/23
Sept	30	18/30	70	14/23
Oct	60	12/21	100	12/20
Nov	120	9/15	130	8/15
Dec	80	5/11	100	6/14

unlucky not to see a raptor of one sort of another and honey buzzards in particular are quite common. On a smaller scale stone-curlew, pin-tailed and black-bellied sandgrouse, European roller, bee-eater, calandra and short-toed lark, and black-eared wheatear, and hoopoe are all present, with Collared pratincole and Gull-billed tern locally in evidence near river valleys and reservoirs. Early in the year, in the south, and on any vertical object, noisy storks will be impossible to miss.

Mammals are less visible, but you will see the black Iberian pigs, which eat acorns and keep the number of oak trees in check, and beautiful herds of brown cattle sheltering in the shade.

CHOOSING YOUR ROUTE

This guidebook presents a choice between Gijón and Santiago de Compostela as final destinations. From the perspective of pilgrimage, the latter is the obvious choice. The journey there takes an extra day, is harder (three passes rather than one) and the intervening towns and cities are not as interesting as those on the way to Gijón. Alternatively, getting across the Cantabrian mountains on the Gijón route on road involves a gentle climb and spectacular descent. The off-road traverse is amazing and the 20km stretch along an old Roman road is one of the highlights of the whole trip.

ACCOMMODATION

The guidebook assumes place-to-place cycling with each day finishing at a town or city, generally with sight-seeing opportunities. There is good-value accommodation all along the route to suit every budget.

The cheapest accommodation is in *albergues* provided for pilgrims. Because they are designed to accommodate walkers these are never that far apart. To get access you'll need a pilgrim's passport, known as the *credenciál* in Spanish, which you can get in Seville or online from a Camino-related group such as the UK's Confraternity of St James. The *albergues* provide dorm-style accommodation exclusively for pilgrims and usually include facilities to wash and dry clothes and sometimes a kitchen. Traditionally, payment in a pilgrim's *albergue* was a donation but this practice is dying out and a fixed charge, rarely more than €10, is now usual.

If you want a room to yourself then for around €30 it's usually possible to find a twin room in a small hotel or bar. These are always spotlessly clean and good fun places to stay.

For those less restricted by budget, and willing to spend between €80 and €100 a night on a twin room, you can stay in a palace. Most of the important destinations on the route have paradors. Paradors are a unique Spanish institution. They were started in the 1920s as a state-owned hotel chain and established to protect historic buildings in need of

Arriving at the parador in León (Stage 11)

restoration. All the paradors are good, some are amazing, with paradors in León, Santiago de Compostela and Plasencia competing with each other for the gold medal. A parador package is available for pilgrims and this secures a 15 per cent discount.

If staying in palaces is your thing, then paradors aren't the only option – the NH chain also provides accommodation in beautifully restored buildings, and if you enjoy superior bathroom products then choose one of these.

Apart from at a couple of stopping points, there is plenty of choice. They can all be found and booked via Booking.com or similar websites. But to get the best price, either phone the accommodation direct or check on the day – web rates can usually be beaten. Accommodation is rarely fully

23

Jamón Ibérico de Bellota

booked unless there is something special going on such as a festival.

As with accommodation, food in Spain is good value and available to suit every budget.

The first challenge is when to eat. One option is to make the Spanish lunch, served until 15.30, the main meal after finishing the day's cycling. So, have breakfast either at the hotel or in a bar, a mid-morning coffee and one or more snacks en route. A big multi-course lunch after a shower on arrival, a post-lunch siesta, sightseeing followed by people-watching in the *plaza mayor* (main square) and tapas makes for an enjoyable daily routine. For non-locals, tapas can be a little confusing as the charging approach changes as you journey north – in the south, it tends to be a complimentary extra with drinks, whereas in the north there might be a small charge – but it is usually a better option than dinner, which generally doesn't start until 21.30.

Spanish is original fusion food, and Arabic and Jewish traditions combine with Spanish and New World influences to produce a distinct cuisine. Meat seems to hit you from every angle, but at the same time Spain prides itself on modern innovative cuisine. Vegetarian food is available but you have to work a bit harder to find it. The cuisine varies by region and there are local specialities, often reinvented in a fresh and modern way, which are well worth trying.

Food in Andalucía is strongly influenced by its Muslim legacy with specialities including *majama* – salt cured tuna (which can be *very* salty), *huevos a la Flamenca* – eggs baked on vegetables and a sauce in a clay pot, or a special Andalucían tomato soup known as *salmorejo*.

Extremadura cuisine is strongly influenced by ingredients from the New World, in particular *pimentón* – paprika brought back by the conquistadors to this part of Spain – and chickpeas. Regional specialities include: *pimentón de la vera* – pork marinated in paprika; *cocido Extremadura* – a chickpea stew with meat, usually chicken; and *cabrito en cuchifrito* – fried baby goat and roast meat. Cáceres is a particular gastronomic hotspot and was recently voted Spain's gastronomy capital.

Castilla y León is Spain's largest region, with lots of specialities. Traditionally chickpeas formed a core component of the cuisine and, like Extremadura, roast meats feature strongly. Look out for *Hornazo* – a meat pie from Salamanca, with a characteristic diagonal-grid pattern on top of the dough, and *Huevas con Farinato* – scrambled eggs with a distinct local sausage, trout and *pimentón* soup in León (particularly at Orbiga just to the south), and garlic soup in Zamora. The Barrio Húmedo Quarter in León has a reputation throughout Spain as the best place to eat tapas.

Both Galicia and Asturias are famous for their seafood, with Asturias particularly well known for its salmon. The most famous dish from Asturias, known throughout Spain and sometimes sold canned, is *Fabada Asturiana*, often referred to simply as *fabada*. It's a rich bean soup with pork, black pudding (*morcilla*), chorizo and saffron. Famous dishes from Galicia, Spain's seafood and dairy larder, include *pulpo a la gallega* – Galician octopus – and *pimientos de Padrón*, small green peppers (originally from Mexico) from the Galician province of Padrón.

The Spanish eat a lot of pork and it seems that everywhere you visit lays claim to the best *jamón*. Production is carefully regulated. There are two grades – Jamón Serrano and Jamón Ibérico. Serrano ham is the standard stuff and accounts for 90 per cent of production, while Jamón Ibérico is the artisan product. There are four grades of Jamón Ibérico depending on how much pure Ibérico pig is involved and the extent to which its diet consists of acorns. The top grade is Jamón Ibérico de Bellota. There are four designated areas which, providing the meat meets the specified grade, can call their ham Jamón Ibérico de Bellota, and all of these areas lie within the *dehesa*.

GETTING THERE

The first decision is whether to take your own bike.

If you are attached to your bike, bear in mind that travelling with it could be a challenge – particularly as the departure and arrival points are

Bike ready for bagging

different, so the obvious option of a heavy-duty bike box – something that should protect all the precious bits – doesn't really work. One tried-and-tested solution is to buy a Cycle Touring Club plastic bag from Wiggle and wrap the bike up in that. The most delicate parts of the bike – such as the rear derailleur and the disc brakes – can be cushioned with lots of bubble wrap protection. Remove the pedals, turn the handlebars, and further protect the derailleur by removing the front wheel and wrapping it against the derailleur (with the disc facing inwards). If your bike has through axles, leave the front one on to protect the front fork.

Be prepared for a variety of responses to your bagged-up bike. A certain amount of chutzpah might be needed to deal with the inevitable negotiations. If it comes to it, you can pay about €15 for a security wrapping service to further secure your bike in miles of plastic. Thus wrapped, it may

well be as robustly protected as by the toughest bike box.

If you are not too concerned about the excess plastic, order a second bag to be delivered to your last hotel. At the very least, this second bag will get further use on a subsequent trip. The alternative is to roll up the original bag and attach it to the bike so it can be reused.

Another option is to get a bike shop to pack your bike for you. In Gijón, Bici-oh on Calle del Carmen will put your bike in a box (recommended if travelling via Asturias Airport) and in Santiago de Compostela, Velocipedo (www.elvelocipedo.com) will pack a bike and organise its onward transportation.

Specialist bike transport services operate from the UK and will organise both dispatch and return using their own packaging. SendBike (www.sendbike.com) will pick a bike up from a home address in the UK and organise its return from a nominated address in Spain.

The other option to consider, particularly if your travel arrangements are complicated, is hiring a bike. One company offering this service that comes well recommended is Bike Iberia, which delivers all sorts of bike (including e-bikes and touring tandems) to your hotel at the beginning of the route and picks it up at the end. Hire rates can be found on its website (www.bikeiberia.com) and represent good value when savings on air baggage are taken into account.

Seville airport is well-served by budget airlines, including easyJet (www.easyjet.com), Ryanair (www.ryanair.com) and Vueling (www.vueling.com), as well as British Airways (www.britishairways.com) and Iberia (www.iberia.com), from a range of destinations in the UK and mainland Europe. The airport is about 10km northeast of the city centre and cyclable. Gijón's nearest airport is Asturias, about 40km to the west, and Santiago de Compostela has its own airport 14km east of the city.

Train travel by bike in Spain has historically been difficult, but is improving and is now a similar challenge to that of taking a bike on a plane. For the latest position see the excellent Seat 61 website (www.seat61.com).

Taking bikes on coaches, however, is straightforward. The coach network in Spain is excellent and most operators accommodate bikes in the luggage compartment. The largest operator, ALSA (www.alsa.com), insists that bikes are bagged and, at a price, bags are provided.

Travelling light

WHAT TO TAKE

Bikepacking mountain bikers have transformed the approach to cycle touring luggage with oversized back saddle bags and front handlebar bags replacing the more traditional pannier approach. Panniers can carry more, but for look and feel, the new approach has a lot going for it. Either way the aim is to keep the load as light as possible.

For cycling gear, taking two of everything that has direct contact with skin is a good rule of thumb. While it should be possible to wash and dry an outfit every night, a back-up is worth the little extra weight. Chances are that the weather is going to be dry, but do take a waterproof top. Also, some sort of midweight fleece or merino long-sleeve jacket can double up as something to wear in the evening. Helmets are required by law in Spain, and most touring cyclists abide by this, although it is rarely enforced. Cycling shoes (MTB style), a cap and gloves are recommended, but a matter of preference.

Pack a pair of lightweight hiking trousers and a couple of T-shirts plus a pair of lightweight trainers for time off the bike. Toiletries should include a first-aid kit, travel wash, lipsalve and suntan lotion.

Essential for most travellers will be a phone, (potentially attached to the bike for navigation) charger and, if the phone camera is not considered adequate, a camera and appropriate battery charger.

For the bike you should have a bell, pump, and drink containers. While it is unlikely you'll need lights, in bad weather they will help make sure you can be seen. There are a few tunnels on the route, but they are illuminated and short. Carry a multi-tool with a chain-repair tool and a spare link and if your bike has one, a spare derailleur hanger (the connector between the derailleur and the frame).

Fabulous dehesa cycling north of Carcaboso (Stage 7)

Take spare inner tubes and a puncture repair kit. The bike chain will need lubrication on a 14-day trip so take some dry-lube.

Most people will also carry a lock. If you plan to stay in hotels you should also be offered secure storage for your bike. If your bike is valuable to you, it may be best to use both.

If new to cycle touring, it would be sensible to complete a bike maintenance course before your journey. With luck, on a 14-day trip, none of the skills acquired should be needed (particularly if the bike is fitted with heavy-duty touring tyres), but a course will build confidence.

The route is well served by cycle shops and bike mechanics are part of a warm, welcoming international fraternity of cycling enthusiasts. No doubt your bike will already be fully serviced and ready to go when you set off for Spain, but if it isn't, getting a service locally in Seville can be incredibly good value.

NAVIGATION

Ruta Vía de la Plata Association way-marking has been placed on some parts of the route, but it is not to the same standard as waymarking on comparable routes on long-distance cycling tracks in France or even the UK. Having said that, navigation is not difficult. On the road legs the combination of road signs and road-side kilometre markers make things easy. The off-road legs are a little more complicated, but the route nearly always follows a well-defined track. Yellow arrow Camino markers generally define the route, and where they do not this is referred to in the text. The Association's La Ruta en Bici app is also useful for navigation.

Finding the hotel at your destination, particularly in one of the larger towns, can be the most frustrating navigational challenge of the day. Make sure you know exactly where it is before arriving and ideally plot it on Google maps and use the Google direction finder for the last few hundred metres. There is nothing worse than roaming around an unknown town, in a hurry for lunch, searching for an obstinately hidden hotel.

Using GPS

While navigation is not difficult, it's still easy to miss a turn. Finding the exit from small towns can be particularly challenging. A GPS attached to the bike enabling the route to be checked while cycling is recommended. A smartphone can be attached to the bike using a mount such as Quad Lock. In terms of GPS apps, of the many available, for this trip consider the free option offered by the Centro Nacional de Información Geográfica Mapas de España (www.cnig.es) which provides access at all scales to the Spanish map base.

The main GPS challenge is learning how to use it and practice should be part of pre-trip preparations. Once mastered, location on the route is easy, and at any time it is possible to establish how far it is to the next coffee or the final destination.

GPX tracks

Whatever GPS you use it will need to be loaded with the route – the GPX file – which provides the line on the map, the route overlay, which can be followed when navigating.

GPX tracks for all stages in this guidebook are available to download free at www.cicerone.co.uk/1012/GPX. GPX files are provided in good faith, but neither the author nor the publisher accept responsibility for their accuracy.

USING THIS GUIDE

The route has been divided into stages corresponding to a day's cycling. Each day finishes in a village, town or city where there is cycling-friendly accommodation and somewhere to eat. The information provided is designed to enable the widest range of cyclists to enjoy the route and describes both on and off-road versions.

Each stage description begins with a **summary box** giving the key statistics for the stage (distance, time, ascent, and descent), followed by an **introduction** positioning the stage within the overall route, describing the landscape, key geographic features and any particular challenges.

In most stages the route description is broken down into **legs**. These are essentially subsections of the

stage and they finish at points where a choice can be made between on- and off-road routes. The **road** route is described first, followed by the **off-road** route. A **hybrid** route is recommended for off-road cyclists who want to cherry-pick the best stages – see the summary box for details of the legs that make up the hybrid route.

Time, for most people, will be a key planning metric, but the time needed to complete a stage will vary enormously from person to person and be influenced by prevailing conditions. Having completed the first couple of stages it should be possible to calibrate the estimates in the guidebook to something closer to your own preferred speed.

Ascent and descent figures are approximate and calculated using the GPS trail and the Spanish map base.

To help riders decide between staying on the off-road route and swapping to the road route, the off-road legs are categorised according to how difficult the leg is and whether it is worth doing.

Four categories of difficulty correspond to:

- **easy:** gravel and flat – wide trails
- **moderate:** gravel with gentle ascents and descents – wide trails
- **difficult:** significant ascents and descents, single track with some walking
- **challenging:** very significant ascents and descents; anticipate some walking and technical stretches

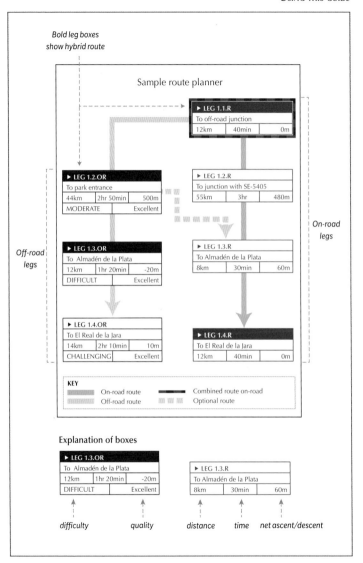

Bold leg boxes
show hybrid route

Sample route planner

▶ LEG 1.1.R
To off-road junction

| 12km | 40min | 0m |

▶ LEG 1.2.OR
To park entrance

| 44km | 2hr 50min | 500m |
| MODERATE | | Excellent |

▶ LEG 1.2.R
To junction with SE-5405

| 55km | 3hr | 480m |

▶ LEG 1.3.OR
To Almadén de la Plata

| 12km | 1hr 20min | -20m |
| DIFFICULT | | Excellent |

▶ LEG 1.3.R
To Almadén de la Plata

| 8km | 30min | 60m |

▶ LEG 1.4.OR
To El Real de la Jara

| 14km | 2hr 10min | 10m |
| CHALLENGING | | Excellent |

▶ LEG 1.4.R
To El Real de la Jara

| 12km | 40min | 0m |

Off-road
legs

On-road
legs

KEY

░░░ On-road route   ▬ Combined route on-road
▨▨▨ Off-road route   ▨ ▨ ▨ Optional route

Explanation of boxes

▶ LEG 1.3.OR
To Almadén de la Plata

| 12km | 1hr 20min | -20m |
| DIFFICULT | | Excellent |

difficulty   quality

▶ LEG 1.3.R
To Almadén de la Plata

| 8km | 30min | 60m |

distance   time   net ascent/descent

31

Passing the time with pilgrims at Baños de Montemayor (Stage 7)

The three quality categories for the off-road legs correspond to:

- **excellent:** unmissable if equipped for off-road
- **good:** to be completed unless short on time
- **poor:** only worth doing if desperate to stay off-road

It should be remembered that generally speaking the off-road route follows the Camino, so riders intent on following the pilgrimage route will need to accept the pitfalls described in order to follow it.

Ride planners

A ride planner is provided for every stage except Stages 13 and 14. This summarises the information for each leg (distance, time, net ascent and descent, and – in the case of the off-road legs – quality and difficulty), and shows where cyclists can swap between the road and off-road routes.

In the sample ride planner shown, cyclists following the road route would do Leg 1.1.R, Leg 1.2.R, Leg 1.3.R and Leg 1.4.R. Those following the off-road route would complete Leg 1.1.R, Leg 1.2.OR, Leg 1.3.OR and Leg 1.4.OR. The recommended hybrid route is shown by the bolded leg boxes and would be Leg 1.1.R Leg 1.2OR, Leg 1.3OR, swapping back to Leg 1.4R to finish.

RUTA VÍA DE LA PLATA

STAGE 1

Seville to El Real de la Jara

Start	Seville
Distance	Road 87km, off-road 82km, hybrid 80km
Ascent	Road 1240m, off-road 1180m
Descent	Road 800m, off-road 740m
Time	Road 4hr 50min, off-road 7hr, hybrid 5hr 30min
Hybrid route	Leg 1.1.R → Leg 1.2.OR → Leg 1.3.OR → Leg 1.4.R

Stage 1 starts at the cathedral and heads north to the small town of El Real de la Jara on the border with Extremadura. El Real de la Jara is perhaps the least interesting of all the destinations on the RVP, which is just as well because if you're taking the off-road route there will be little energy left for post-cycling perambulations.

Apart from two ridges on the off-road route, altitude is gained gently. Leaving the coastal plain and entering Parque Natural de la Sierra Norte Sevilla results in a change in landscape, with the stunning *dehesa*, characteristic of the middle stages of the RVP, experienced for the first time.

The Ruta Vía de la Plata Association recommends El Real de la Jara as the stage end, but nearby Almadén de la Plata offers slightly better choices for both accommodation and places to eat. Of course, staying there makes for a longer Stage 2.

Road cyclists on Stage 1 get their first taste of the N-630 which, at the beginning, is a little busier than is typical. Not everyone likes cycling on a hard shoulder but it's a big one and generally free of gravel and debris. About half of the route is on the N-630 and half on even quieter country roads. Although the motorway is never far away, and crossed several times, it's not intrusive.

Stage 1 is a wonderful introduction to the off-road delights of the RVP, offering plenty of variety, with 57 of its 82km off-road. Net ascent for the day is about 550m (1200m up and 700m down) and there are climbs on Leg 3 and 4 where most people will need to walk with their bike. There are three towns along the route where breaks can be taken and lunch found.

This is a long stage so it is recommended that you drop the challenging last off-road leg and take the road route into El Real de la Jara. This reduces the time needed for the stage from 7hr to 5hr 30min. For an even easier hybrid option, one which avoids a tough climb and descent at the end of Off-Road Leg 3, consider continuing along the road from Castiblancos de los Arroyos to join the road route into Almadén de la Plata.

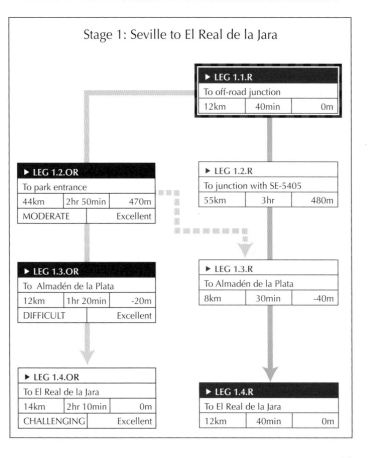

Stage 1: Seville to El Real de la Jara

▶ LEG 1.1.R

To off-road junction		
12km	40min	0m

▶ LEG 1.2.OR

To park entrance		
44km	2hr 50min	470m
MODERATE		Excellent

▶ LEG 1.2.R

To junction with SE-5405		
55km	3hr	480m

▶ LEG 1.3.OR

To Almadén de la Plata		
12km	1hr 20min	-20m
DIFFICULT		Excellent

▶ LEG 1.3.R

To Almadén de la Plata		
8km	30min	-40m

▶ LEG 1.4.OR

To El Real de la Jara		
14km	2hr 10min	0m
CHALLENGING		Excellent

▶ LEG 1.4.R

To El Real de la Jara		
12km	40min	0m

SEVILLE

Plaza de España, Seville

Most people will have a night in Seville before setting off and, buzzing and bustling, it's a wonderful place. The capital of Andalucía, there is lots to see and do in Spain's fourth-largest city (population 690,000).

The historic core of the city, on the eastern banks of the Guadalquivir, contains buildings that reflect the city's pre-Roman origins and subsequent development by Muslims and Christians after the reconquest (1248). Seville rose to international prominence after Christopher Columbus reached the Americas, becoming the gateway to the wealth that flowed into Europe from Spain's growing empire. Three important buildings; all UNESCO World Heritage Sites, reflect the city's development. The Alcázar Palace complex was built on the site of a Muslim fortress shortly after the reconquest and is the most important example of Mudéjar architecture (a fusion of Muslim and Gothic styles) in Spain. The cathedral is the third largest in the world, and although predominantly Gothic in style, its interior and floorplan are based on its antecedent as a mosque. Particularly impressive is the bell tower, originally a minaret, which can be climbed by a horse with rider. The cathedral contains the tomb of Christopher Columbus. The third building – the General Archive of the Indies – was originally built as a sort of stock exchange to accommodate merchants handling trade from the New World. Commissioned by Phillip II in 1572 in Renaissance style, the building now houses all the original documentation associated with Spain's overseas possessions.

With the silting up of the Guadalquivir, and the shift of the port downriver to Cadiz, Seville's Golden Age ended and the city, like Spain as a whole, suffered something of a post-imperial hangover.

Seville is now a busy place and a magnet for tourists who combine visits to its Alcázar Palace complex and cathedral with trips to Cordoba and Granada. Given the challenge ahead, cyclists will probably not attempt to see everything, but an early evening walk around the old town – finding the RVP departure point at the cathedral – is recommended.

There are lots of places to stay and eat in Seville, but to sample the atmosphere and the city's legendary tapas try to find somewhere in the Alameda or Macarons districts to the north of the city centre.

ROAD ROUTE

Leg 1.1.R to off-road junction

Escaping Seville is the worst part of the day. For a good start-of-trip photograph consider the huge northern door of the cathedral. Head west across the junction down past the bullring and cross the Puente de Isabel II into the Triana district. Take the third right after the bridge along a main road and then take a left turn at a junction with the Calle Castilla. Turn right at the next junction and use the traffic lights to cross a dual carriageway to a cycle path – the worst part is now behind

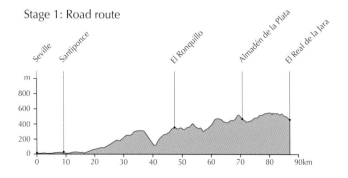

Stage 1: Road route

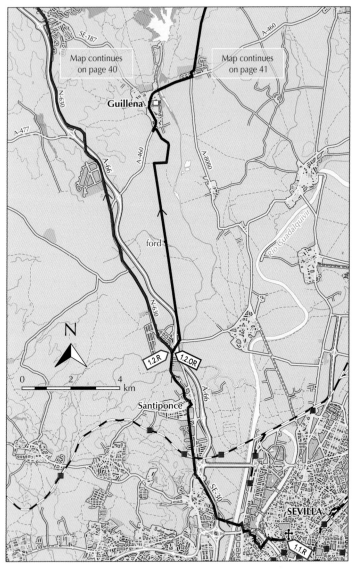

Map continues on page 40

Map continues on page 41

you. At the roundabout take the scruffy cycle path on the far side of the first exit and after about 90 metres head down into a car park where, on some large concrete pipes, are yellow Camino arrows. Cross a bridge over the Río Guadalquivir, pass under a major road, turn sharp right and head north to a major traffic junction just to the south of **Santiponce**. Take the Santiponce exit at the roundabout, continue north through the town to another roundabout where the road and off-road legs head off in different directions.

Leg 1.2.R to junction with SE-5405
Join the N-630 at the roundabout to the north of Santiponce and follow it for 38km to **El Ronquillo** where there are lots of places for refreshments. The route is undulating, climbing 300m, before losing most of the gain and then climbing again before El Ronquillo. At a junction with the motorway 5km to the north of El Ronquillo join the A-8175 and follow the signs to Almadén de la Plata. It's another 8km to the junction with the off-road variant (following SE-5405).

Leg 1.3.R to Almadén de la Plata
There is a small climb on the road route just before reaching **Almadén de la Plata** but nothing to compare to the off-road route.

Leg 1.4.R to El Real de la Jara
Head east out of Almadén de la Plata. At the junction after 2km, turn left and follow the road, climbing gently and then descending, north and then east into **El Real de la Jara**.

OFF-ROAD (CAMINO) ROUTE

Leg 1.1.R to off-road junction
Follow Leg 1.1.R as described in the road route.

Leg 1.2.OR to park entrance
The off-road route presents an abrupt change of mood and, after the mess of Seville's urban fringe, follows the Camino into a wide-open landscape.

Follow the A-8079 under the motorway and after a few metres take a sharp left onto a straight agricultural track. Follow it north for 8km. Halfway along, the track **fords a stream** which early in the year will be full. If it is, use the footbridge hidden away to the right in bushes. Turn right at the end of the straight stretch and then left, taking a path around the edge of a field to a main road, turn right and head into **Guillena**, a potential refreshment stop.

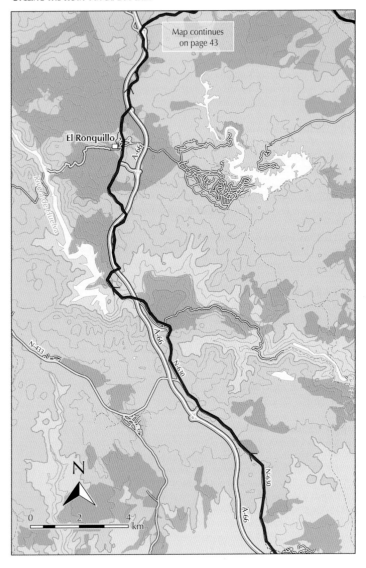

Map continues
on page 43

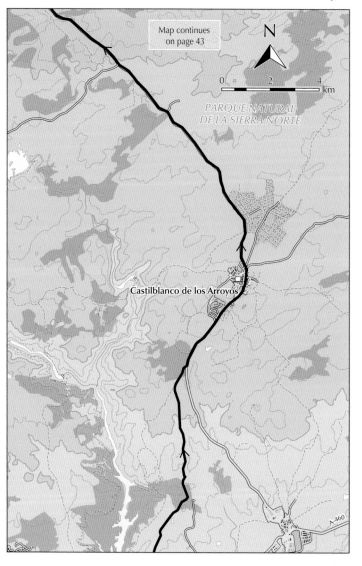

Map continues
on page 43

N

0   2   4
km

*PARQUE NATURAL
DE LA SIERRA NORTE*

Castilblanco de los Arroyos

A-460

Stage 1: Off-road route

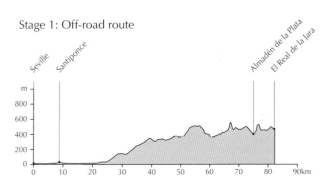

If, after your first taste of RVP off-road cycling, you decide that the road route is preferable, it can be found by following the SE-187 northeast out of town for 4km to rejoin the road route.

To continue off-road follow the main road east out of town turning left after 1.5km through a small scruffy industrial estate onto an agricultural track. Follow the track north for 11km to a road. This stretch of cycling is good, but tougher than the first. It is climbing, the track is a little overgrown in places, and occasionally the topsoil has been washed away leaving exposed bedrock.

First taste of off-road

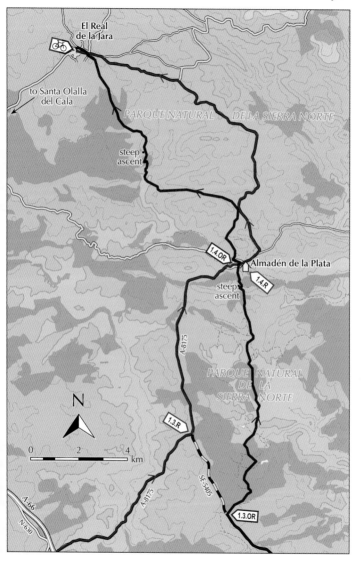

First day in the dehesa

Turn right onto a road and head into **Castilblanco de los Arroyos**, another potential refreshment stop. Take a sharp left immediately to the north of the town and follow a road for 15km climbing 200m. The end of the leg is marked by a junction with an agricultural road with information boards for the park, the Parque Natural de la Sierra Norte Sevilla. To avoid the steep climb at the end of the next off-road leg, stay on the road to join the road route.

Leg 1.3.OR to Almadén de la Plata

This stunning stretch of cycling, still following the Camino, has a sting in the tail, a savage climb over a ridge just south of Almadén de la Plata.

Head through the park entrance and follow a dirt track for 1.5km, bear left through farm buildings and continue north for another 4km. Turn left at a junction, head through buildings on a low rise and continue north for another 4km to the ridge. Here the bike will need to be pushed for 100m or so before descending from the pass on a concrete track into **Almadén de la Plata**.

> If stopping at **Almadén de la Plata** as an alternative to El Real de la Jara, consider the Hotel El Romeral, which has the best restaurant, or the Hostal Restaurante Casa Concha, just across the road. Pilgrimage-style accommodation can be found at the municipal *albergue* (tel +34 692 735 043).

Leg 1.4.OR to El Real de la Jara

The final off-road leg includes some excellent *dehesa* landscape but passes through lots of small holdings where the goats, sheep, cattle and pigs are sometimes guarded by large intimidating dogs. It also involves difficult stretches of track where steep ascents will necessitate walking. After a long first day, the recommended hybrid route avoids the last off-road leg.

Following the Camino signs, head past the church in Almadén de la Plata and west out of town. About 200m from the church take a right turn and go north, climbing past the town's water tank. Continue on an agricultural road, through farmsteads for 1km to where the route leaves the road and joins a stretch of single track. Follow this track to where it almost meets the main road (and the road route) before swinging west and joining another agricultural road. Continue west through multiple gates for 3km, turn north and embark on a **steep 150m climb** on a difficult trail, occasionally single track. At the pass, join a dirt road and follow it into **El Real de la Jara**.

EL REAL DE LA JARA

El Real de la Jara

'Real', in this context, means royal and refers to the fact that Alfonso XI stayed here in 1340 before beating the Moroccan Marinids dynasty at the Battle of Río Salado in 1340. The town's main feature is a medieval castle, beautifully illuminated in the evening. For accommodation, cheap but primitive, consider the Hostal La Encina or the Alojamiento Mo Carmen which, although not as nice, is nearer to the Meson la Cochera, the best place to eat. Both places can be found on Booking.com. For pilgrimage-style accommodation go to the municipal *albergue* (tel +34 954 733 007) or a private *albergue* (tel +34 654 862 553).

STAGE 2
El Real de la Jara to Zafra

Start	El Real de la Jara
Distance	Road 90km, off-road 77km, hybrid 77km
Ascent	Road 740m, off-road 710m
Descent	Road 700m, off-road 670m
Time	Road 4hr 55min, off-road 6hr, hybrid 5hr 40min
Hybrid route	Leg 2.1.OR → Leg 2.2.R → Leg 2.3.OR

On Stage 2 the RVP leaves Andalucía, crosses the watershed between the Guadalquivir and the Guadiana and starts its long journey through Extremadura. The landscape mixes stunning *dehesa* with the wide-open spaces of the *meseta* and, apart from one 250m climb, both road and off-road follow non-challenging routes. The road route is 13km longer than the more direct off-road route, although the off-road route involves more climb and descent. The short middle leg of the off-road route, which follows a scruffy track alongside the motorway up a steep 250m hill is best avoided, and the recommended hybrid route reverts to the road route. Among other things, this leaves more time for refreshments in Monesterio, the town just beyond the ridge.

There is plenty to see in Zafra and although there are lunch options en route, Stage 2 is a good opportunity to practice the late lunch strategy described in the Introduction.

ROAD ROUTE

Leg 2.1.R to junction with off-road
Head west out of town for 9km to the N-630 **Santa Olalla de Cala**, another small town with bars and a few shops – the next coffee is 22km away. Continue north out of the town on the N630 and after 5km follow it underneath the motorway. Continue for another 10km to another motorway interchange and start of the climb to Monesterio.

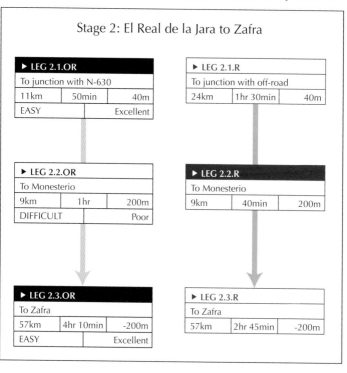

Stage 2: El Real de la Jara to Zafra

▶ LEG 2.1.OR		
To junction with N-630		
11km	50min	40m
EASY		Excellent

▶ LEG 2.1.R		
To junction with off-road		
24km	1hr 30min	40m

▶ LEG 2.2.OR		
To Monesterio		
9km	1hr	200m
DIFFICULT		Poor

▶ LEG 2.2.R		
To Monesterio		
9km	40min	200m

▶ LEG 2.3.OR		
To Zafra		
57km	4hr 10min	-200m
EASY		Excellent

▶ LEG 2.3.R		
To Zafra		
57km	2hr 45min	-200m

Stage 2: Road route

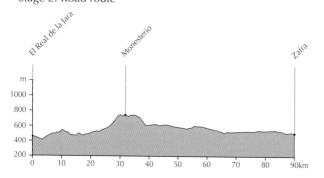

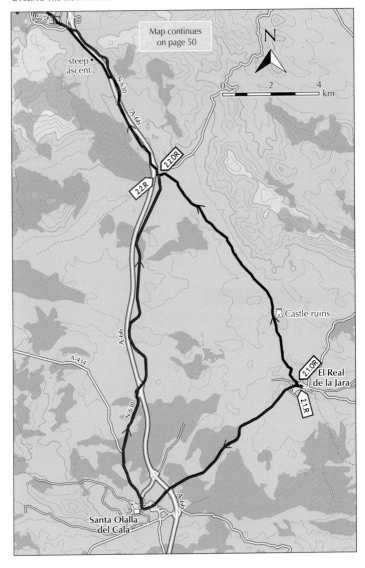

Map continues on page 50

48

Leg 2.2.R to Monesterio
The climb to the top of the pass is 230m, but the road, designed for heavy vehicles, is nicely graded and easily managed. From the top it's a short run down into **Monesterio** and, if the temptations of the Jamon Museum can be resisted, the chance for coffee and *tosta e jamón*.

Leg 2.3.R to Zafra
The road route to Zafra is fast and easy, skirting all the towns and villages visited in the off-road route. Follow the N-630 from kilometre marker 721 to 786, then turn left onto a country road to **Puebla de Sancho Pérez** and on into **Zafra**. Stay on this road until it reaches a municipal park, turn left and immediately right and head to the end of the street and the walls of the town's historic core.

OFF-ROAD (CAMINO) ROUTE

Leg 2.1.OR to junction with N-630
Using Camino markers, follow the road at the western side of the church north to its end and turn left (the castle will be above you on the right). Join an agriculture road and follow it for 11km. Watch out for the **ruins of a castle** which should appear about 1km after leaving the town.

Leg 2.2.OR to Monesterio
This leg is the first of several on the overall route where the road and off-routes run side by side and where the ugliness of the off-road route and the emptiness of the road route make the road more appealing. What makes it particularly messy is the proximity of the motorway. For the first 2km the route follows a narrow

Stage 2: Off-road route

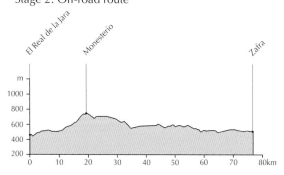

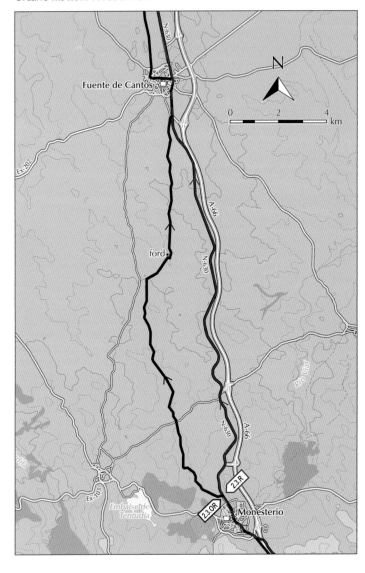

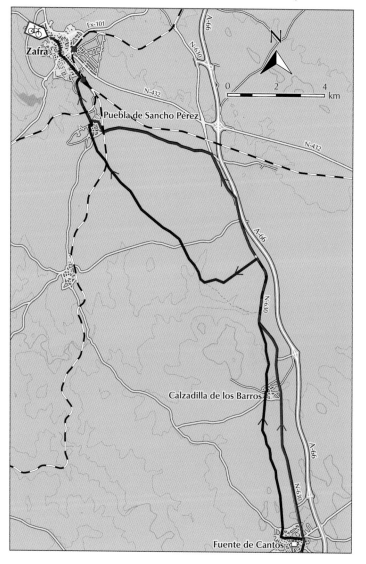

strip of land between the N-630 and the motorway, passes underneath the motorway, joins a lane consisting of building rubble at the bottom of the motorway embankment, makes a steep climb to a pass, and rejoins the N-630 heading into **Monesterio**.

Leg 2.3.OR to Zafra

The road and off-road run close to each other almost all the way to Zafra and it's possible to swap onto the road route at various places if time is short or a little more comfort is preferred. The off-road route, however, is excellent and presents no serious challenges.

To find the start, continue along the N-630 to the northern edge of Monesterio and turn left onto an agricultural road north of a football pitch. Follow this descending road and take the left-hand fork over a stream. Continue north, crossing a road after 2km, along a track that forms a boundary between the *dehesa* on

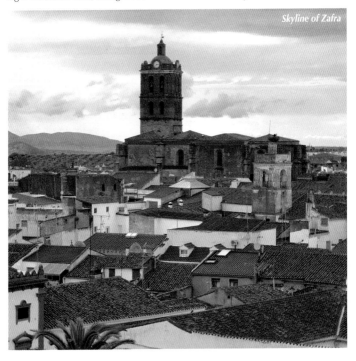

Skyline of Zafra

the left and open landscape on the right. After 7km the *dehesa* ends and the route descends down through enormous fields to a stream and a **ford**. Cross the stream (expect wet feet) and continue north on a climbing track for 6km to the N-630 (leaving the Camino signs) and head toward **Fuente de Cantos**.

Fuente de Cantos is a densely packed, substantial little town with all the usual amenities, and finding the route out of it is a challenge without GPS. The route leaves the town (following Camino signs) near its northwest corner, crossing a street forming the northern boundary of the town, the Calle Fernando Poo, opposite a small church.

Head north for 5km, pass through the village of **Calzadilla de los Barros** and continue for 4km to the N-630. The Camino turns off the N-630 after 200m but the route, to avoid fords, follows the N-630 for 3km and takes a left-hand turn onto an agricultural track heading west. The turn is about 800m after the 691 kilometre marker so if you see the 692 marker you've gone too far. Follow this track west for 2km, turn right to rejoin the Camino and follow it for 8km to **Puebla de Sancho Pérez**. Find the main road to the north of the village and follow it for 4km to **Zafra**.

ZAFRA

Zafra, the first overnight stop in Extremadura, is a tightly packed town (population 17,000) whose shady, intimate squares (the Plaza Grande and the linked Plaza Chica) are ideal for a post-ride drink.

Originally a Muslim fort, it needed to be captured twice in the 13th century before final occupation by the Christians. For an insight into the history of the Zafra and the life of nuns visit the Museum of the Convent of Santa Maria, a wonderful 15th-century building, hidden just off the main street.

Zafra is particularly proud of Ruy Lópes de Segura who was born in the town and wrote one the first books on chess. He was the world chess champion of his day – until he was beaten by an Italian in 1575.

The parador is located in the town's most monumental building, the El Alcázar, on the outside a fortress and inside a palace. For more intimate accommodation, but just as grand, consider the Casa Palacio Conde de la Corte Hotel, an amazing 19th-century building much favoured by visiting bullfighters. The town has lots of hotels but the medium-priced Hotel Adarve, built into the town's walls, can be vouched for while San Francisco Convent Hostel (tel +34 691 53 72 83) provides pilgrimage-style accommodation.

STAGE 3
Zafra to Mérida

Start	Zafra
Distance	Road 63km, off-road 63km, hybrid 63km
Ascent	Road 350m, off-road 410m
Descent	Road 640m, off-road 700m
Time	Road 3hr 45min, off-road 4hr 50min, hybrid 4hr 50min
Hybrid route	Same as off-road route

Stage 3 is an easy stage, which is good because there is lots to see in Mérida. After a small initial climb the route descends gently all the way to the Río Guadiana and crosses the river into Mérida on the world's longest remaining Roman bridge. The landscape itself is not that interesting, and as pilgrims slog their way across huge, featureless vineyards the benefits of a bike become self-evident. Both road and off-road routes are about 63km and descending. Excluding breaks, the off-road route will take around five hours and the road route about an hour less, so a late lunch in Mérida makes sense as a refreshment strategy.

The route breaks down into four legs with the off-road route and road routes merging for 10km at Torremejía. The off-road legs follow easy agricultural roads. There are two places to stop for refreshments en route and a coffee in the picturesque square in front of the church in Villafranca de los Barros is recommended.

ROAD ROUTE

Leg 3.1.R to off-road junction
From the roundabout immediately to the south of the parador, head east along the main road to another roundabout, the junction with the N-432. Cross the roundabout and follow a climbing road for 6km to the **N-630**. Continue north to the outskirts of Villafranco de los Barros. If it's too early for coffee, Almendralejo is another 14km.

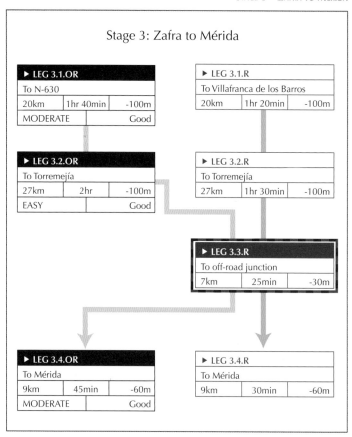

Stage 3: Zafra to Mérida

▶ LEG 3.1.OR		
To N-630		
20km	1hr 40min	-100m
MODERATE		Good

▶ LEG 3.1.R		
To Villafranca de los Barros		
20km	1hr 20min	-100m

▶ LEG 3.2.OR		
To Torremejía		
27km	2hr	-100m
EASY		Good

▶ LEG 3.2.R		
To Torremejía		
27km	1hr 30min	-100m

▶ LEG 3.3.R		
To off-road junction		
7km	25min	-30m

▶ LEG 3.4.OR		
To Mérida		
9km	45min	-60m
MODERATE		Good

▶ LEG 3.4.R		
To Mérida		
9km	30min	-60m

Leg 3.2.R to Torremejía
From the exit to Villafranca de los Barros the N-630 runs close – occasionally very close – to the motorway all the way to **Torremejía,** leaving briefly to visit **Almendralejo**.

Leg 3.3.R to off-road junction
Continue along the N-630 north for about 7km. The turn-off to the off-road route on the Camino is at the top of a rise near the 632 kilometre marker.

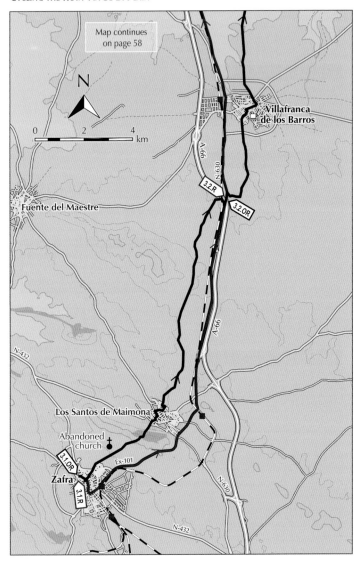

Stage 3: Road route

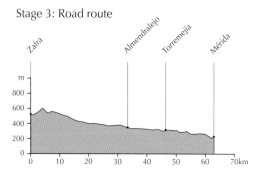

Leg 3.4.R to Mérida

Stay on the N-630 to **Mérida**. On the edge of town turn abruptly east at a rounda-bout. Continue for about 100m then take the third exit from a roundabout, leaving the N-630, and head via the Avenue de Portugal into the city, crossing the river via the Roman bridge.

OFF-ROAD (CAMINO) ROUTE

Leg 3.1.OR to N630

Using the parador in Zafra as the starting point, go north along the Calle López Asme, turn right in front of the large Albergue Convento de San Francisco and head northeast along the Calle Anche. Continue to the edge of town; cross the N-432 via a roundabout, and, using the Camino signs, follow a road up a hill, past

Stage 3: Off-road route

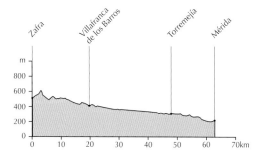

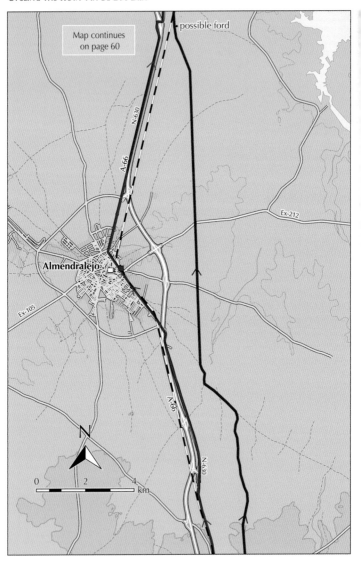

Map continues
on page 60

possible ford

N-630

A-66

Ex-212

Almendralejo

Ex-105

A-66

N-630

N

0   2   4 km

Off-road to Torremejía

an abandoned church reaching the highest point of the day after 3km. From the pass the route descends steeply down to the village of **Los Santos to Maimona**.

Head through the village to a main road on the northern side, turn right and then left following the signs north along the Calle Santisimo. After 500m bear right and continue north along a lovely track for 9km to where the route turns sharply right, climbs onto the N-630 and crosses the motorway.

Leg 3.2.OR to Torremejía

Follow the N-630 north for about 400m, join a track on the right, follow it for 600m, turn north and head into **Villafranca de los Barros**. Finding the exit from Villafranca de los Barros is tricky. Follow the one-way system on the right-hand side of the town centre church to a main road and a small square; then turn left. Continue north-west for 1km into countryside, passing a college, school and playing fields, to a road. Cross the road and continue north on a track for 25km through what must be the world's biggest vineyard. Depending on the weather and the time of year, there might be a stream to **ford** just before the end near a railway. This railway is crossed via a bridge before heading into **Torremejía**. The cafés in Torremejía are on the N-630 which runs through the middle of the little town.

59

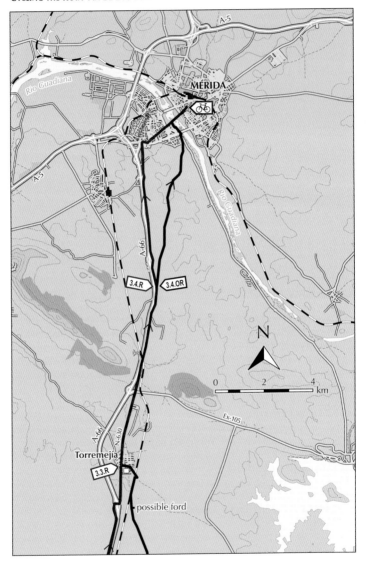

Leg 3.3.R to off-road junction

From Torremejía, join the road and follow Leg 3.3.R as described in the road route.

Leg 3.4.OR to Mérida

The Camino continues down a track leading to what looks like a recycling plant. Keep to the left of the plant and follow an agricultural track, initially poorly defined but soon very pleasant, all the way to **Mérida**. You may meet shepherds with huge flocks of goats, and dogs that are happily well under control. At the end of the track, cross a road and follow a cycle path north along the banks of the Río Guadiana and then leave it to enter the city via the Roman bridge.

MÉRIDA

There is more to Mérida than its Roman legacy, but that legacy is epic and on an almost overwhelming scale. The Roman remains are among the largest in Spain and have UNESCO World Heritage Site status.

Although there is evidence of pre-Roman occupation, it was the Romans who identified Mérida's strategic importance. In 25BC Augustus established a colony there for retired legionnaires. Located at the southern end of the Roman Ruta Vía de la Plata it grew and became

The world's longest Roman bridge at Mérida

the capital of Lusitania, a province that included all of southeastern Iberia. Mérida survived the fall of the Roman Empire and for a time the Visigoths made it their Hispanic capital. In 713 the Muslims came and built a huge fortification, the Alcazaba, at the eastern end of the Roman bridge. Today the city has a population of 60,000 people and is the capital of Extremadura.

There is a lot to take in, but fortunately the amphitheatre (seating capacity 15,000), Roman theatre and a stunning museum are all part of the same complex and most of it can be seen in a couple of hours. After taking in the highlights, stroll down to the temple to the Goddess Diana, the forum and main square for some people-watching and tapas.

There is plenty of accommodation in Mérida, including the parador located in a former 18th-century convent. Similar to the parador, but with a rooftop swimming pool and an even better location, is the Mérida Palace.

Pilgrim accommodation is available at the Albergue de Peregrinos Molino de Pancaliente (tel +34 682 51 43 66), a municipal hostel located on the eastern bank of the river, north of the Roman bridge.

For food, consider the Rex Numitor restaurant located near the Alcazaba. It's a family-run business serving local Extremadura cuisine and producing its own *jamón*.

The amphitheatre in Mérida

STAGE 4
Mérida to Cáceres

Start	Mérida
Distance	Road 69km, off-road 78km, hybrid 78km
Ascent	Road 640m, off-road 750m
Descent	Road 420m, off-road 530m
Time	Road 4hr 25min, off-road 6hr 55min, hybrid 6hr 25min
Hybrid route	Leg 4.1.R → Leg 4.2.OR → Leg 4.3.OR → Leg 4.4.R → Leg 4.5.OR → Leg 4.6.R → Leg 4.7.OR

Hopefully by Stage 4 everything – body and bike – is working in perfect harmony and, after the delights of Mérida, ready to cope with a more challenging stage. The road route to Cáceres is brisk and non-challenging, the off-road option less so. The recommended hybrid route drops the least attractive off-road sections and means Cáceres is less than five-and-a-half hours away.

Leg 2 offers the best off-road cycling when the route dives deep into the *dehesa*. It's fabulous, particularly the first part to Aljucén. Although not as pretty, the cycling after Aldea del Cano is also interesting, including a stretch along a clearly defined Cañada Reales. Escaping the valley formed by the Río Guadiana does involve a bit of climbing and the main ascent is on the approach to Alcuéscar.

Like Mérida, Cáceres is another destination where there is lots to see, so again try to arrive in time for lunch. There are three places to stop for refreshments and although Alcuéscar is the obvious place to stop, time could be saved by missing the town and heading down the hill to Aldea del Cano.

ROAD ROUTE

Leg 4.1.R to off-road junction
To make sure you don't forget that Mérida was one of Spain's most important Roman cities, you visit a stunning Roman aqueduct and the reservoir that supplied it as you leave.

Stage 4: Mérida to Cáceres

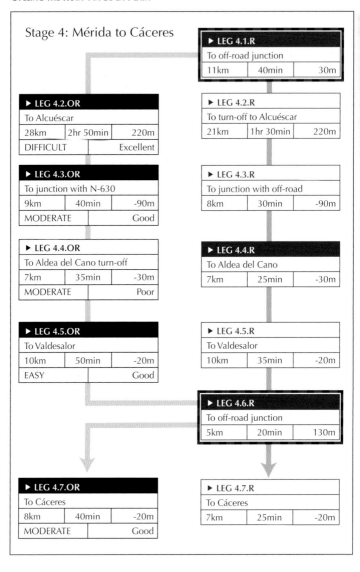

► LEG 4.1.R

To off-road junction

11km	40min	30m

► LEG 4.2.OR

To Alcuéscar

28km	2hr 50min	220m
DIFFICULT		Excellent

► LEG 4.2.R

To turn-off to Alcuéscar

21km	1hr 30min	220m

► LEG 4.3.OR

To junction with N-630

9km	40min	-90m
MODERATE		Good

► LEG 4.3.R

To junction with off-road

8km	30min	-90m

► LEG 4.4.OR

To Aldea del Cano turn-off

7km	35min	-30m
MODERATE		Poor

► LEG 4.4.R

To Aldea del Cano

7km	25min	-30m

► LEG 4.5.OR

To Valdesalor

10km	50min	-20m
EASY		Good

► LEG 4.5.R

To Valdesalor

10km	35min	-20m

► LEG 4.6.R

To off-road junction

5km	20min	130m

► LEG 4.7.OR

To Cáceres

8km	40min	-20m
MODERATE		Good

► LEG 4.7.R

To Cáceres

7km	25min	-20m

Passing the aqueduct leaving Mérida

Using the parador as a starting point go north along the Calle Vespasiano, turning left at the end onto the Calle Marquesa de Pinares. After 200m turn right into a park and follow the signs down to the aqueduct. The route goes round the park leaving it immediately to the west of the aqueduct. Head north from the exit along a small road, take the second exit at the first roundabout and the third exit at the second one (not the main road) and continue northeast, crossing two more roundabouts. Continue out of the city along an empty road (there is a superfluous cycle path running alongside the road). Some 6km from Mérida you come to the reservoir, the **Embalse de Proserpina**, and the low Roman dam on its western side. Continue north for another 4km along a quiet road – the off-road turn-off can be found on a bend as the road swings east.

Leg 4.2.R to turn-off to Alcuéscar

Continue east for 2km and join the N-630, after crossing a bridge over the motorway, near the 612 kilometre marker. For refreshments leave the main road after 6km and head into **Aljucén**. Just past Aljucén, the N-630 crosses the Río

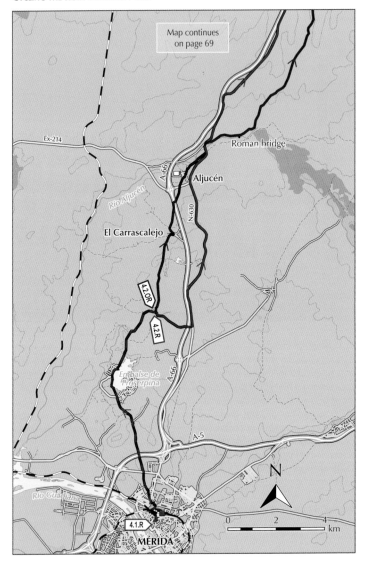

Map continues
on page 69

Ex-214

Roman bridge

Aljucén

Río Aljucén

El Carrascalejo

4.2.0R

4.2.R

Embalse de
Proserpina

A-66

A-5

N

Río Guadiana

4.1.R

MÉRIDA

0   2   4
km

Stage 4: Road route

Aljucén and starts a 200m climb to a pass and turn-off to **Alcuéscar**. If missing out Alcuéscar stay on the N-630 and make the 13km descent to Aldea del Cano.

Leg 4.3.R to junction with off-road
Continue from the pass on a steady descent for 8km to the junction.

Leg 4.4.R to Aldea del Cano
The Las Vegas in **Aldea del Cano**, on the right-hand side of the N-630, and reached just after passing a tiny **Roman bridge**, is ideally located for refreshments.

Leg 4.5.R to Valdesalor
Continue north on an easy, flat N-630 to **Valdesalor**. Look out for 15th-century **Castle Arguijuela**, built on a hilltop near the 569 kilometre marker. It's now a wedding venue.

Leg 4.6.R to off-road junction
Continue along the N-630 and go over an intersection with the motorway, from the 565 kilometre marker to the 560 kilometre marker and the junction with the off-road route.

Leg 4.7.R to Cáceres
Continue on the N-630 across a series of roundabouts to a roundabout near the main train station. Take the second exit to another roundabout reached after 1km, cross it and follow a wide boulevard with a central strip of greenery, cross a busy intersection and head into what is the west side of the **Cáceres'** historic town centre.

Stage 4: Off-road route

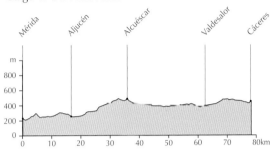

OFF-ROAD (CAMINO) ROUTE

Leg 4.1.R to off-road junction
For the first leg, follow Leg 4.1.R as described in the road route.

Leg 4.2.OR to Alcuéscar
Following Camino signs, head north for 3km along a level track through a stunning landscape to a small village, **El Carrascalejo**. Turn right into the village and then left after 100m back onto an agricultural track; continue north for 1km passing underneath the motorway. Continue into **Aljucén** where refreshments are available. From the village, follow a road downhill to the N-630,

Cycling paradise, north of Mérida

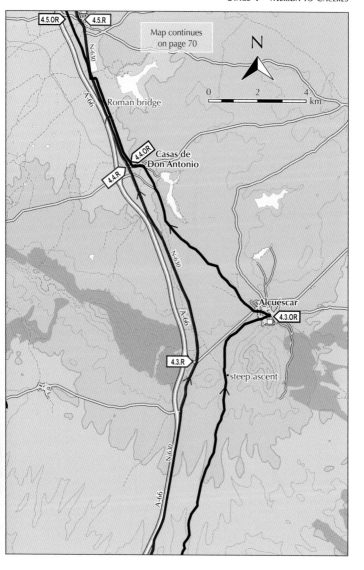

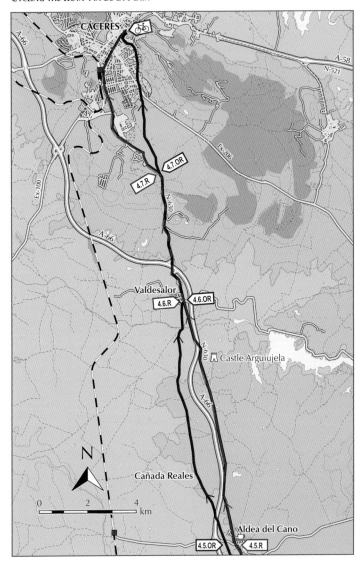

turn left onto it, cross a bridge and take a sharp right. Follow a riverside track east for 2km (perhaps stopping for pictures at a **Roman bridge**) before turning north. Continue along a well-defined path with occasional information boards for 12km, climbing some 200m to a pass. Parts of the track are steep, particularly near the top, and some pushing might be required. From the pass, the route swings east and heads into **Alcuéscar**, 4km away. If missing out Alcuéscar, follow the Camino signs.

Leg 4.3.OR to junction with N-630

From the centre of Alcuéscar head downhill north-west along the Avenida Constitución to a junction with a larger road; cross it and join an agricultural track. Following Camino signs, stay on the track for about 8km to the village of **Casas de Don Antonio**, turn left onto the road and head to the N-630.

Leg 4.4.OR to Aldea del Cano turn-off

The off-road route runs next to N-630 for 4km on its right-hand side, crosses it, and runs almost parallel to it on the left. Other than a picturesque Roman bridge, it's tedious and, particularly if you plan to stop in Aldea del Cano, best avoided.

Leg 4.5.OR to Valdesalor

If Leg 4.4 has been avoided, take the first left off the N-630 at Aldea del Cano, go west along the road for 400m and turn right onto an agricultural track. Continue north through a scrubby landscape (passing underneath the motorway after 1km) guided by the distinct lines of the **Cañada Reales**, 95m wide and marked in various places along the track. Some 3km from the motorway, cross an abandoned aerodrome and continue north for 6km to **Valdesalor**, a dense modern suburb dumped on a flat landscape.

Leg 4.6.R to off-road junction

Join the road and follow Leg 4.6.R as described in the road route.

Leg 4.7.OR to Cáceres

Follow a well-defined track (along another Cañades Reales) for 4km across a treeless upland area, entering **Cáceres** through a rundown industrial park on its southern edge. Continue north on the road to the east of a group of buildings to a bigger road. Immediately on the other side of this road is the Ronda de San Francisco which can be followed to the historic town centre.

CÁCERES

Cáceres (pop 96,000) is famous for both its medieval buildings (it is a World Heritage Site and was a location for *Game of Thrones*) and its Extremadurian cuisine (it was designated Spain's gastronomic capital in 2015).

The Romans established the town in 25BC (there was probably a prehistoric settlement there as well) and, after falling into decline under the Visigoths, it was developed by the Muslims who fortified it, built palaces and numerous towers. It changed hands several times before it was finally secured by the Christians, and then enjoyed a particularly prosperous period during the reconquest and the discovery of the Americas.

It's the concentration of medieval buildings that makes Cáceres special. Narrow winding streets connecting intimate squares surround the most monumental feature, the stunning Plaza Mayor. The square is on the northern side of the citadel and its southern side is formed by the city wall and the Moorish Torre de Bujaco. The stairs and the arch next to the tower takes you through to the Gothic Cathedral de Santa María and the beautiful Plaza de Santa María, with Renaissance buildings and the Palacio de los Golfines de Abajo. With new delights around every corner, the medieval town centre lends itself to relaxed strolling. If you have time, visit both the Palacio de los Golfines de Abajo and the cathedral. Make sure you climb the cathedral tower. The views over the city and the huge expanse of the countryside to the north are wonderful.There are plenty of places to stay. The Parador de Cáceres is located in a beautiful Renaissance palace near the Plaza Mayor.

Cáceres was one of the filming locations for **Game of Thrones**

View over the rooftops of Cáceres

Accommodation in another beautifully restored building can be found nearby at the Palacio de Oquendo just around the corner. Also well located, and cheaper, is the Hotel Albarragena. For budget accommodation consider the El Albergue Ciudad de Cáceres to the northeast of the town centre.

Food is excellent in Cáceres, particularly if you like modern interpretations of tapas. La Minerva located in the Plaza Mayor or La Cacharrería, hidden away near the cathedral are both good. If you have plenty of money and are organised enough to book some time in advance then you could stay at the Atrio hotel and eat in its 2 Michelin star restaurant.

Michelin inspectors don't seem to go to *churros* cafés but if they did they would probably give the Churrería Hnos. Ruiz a least a star. They provide a highly calorific snack in the form of deep-fried pastry, seriously unhealthy, but a Spanish institution. The Churrería Hnos. Ruiz can be found on way out town and the *churrería* is probably the best one on the whole of the RVP.

STAGE 5
Cáceres to Grimaldo

Start	Cáceres
Distance	Road 52km, off-road 53km, hybrid 52km
Ascent	Road 650m, off-road 640m
Descent	Road 620m, off-road 610m
Time	Road 3hr 30min, off-road 5hr 20min, hybrid 4hr 10min
Hybrid route	Leg 5.1.R → Leg 5.2.OR → Leg 5.3.OR → Leg 5.4.R → Leg 5.5.OR → Leg 5.6.R

Stage 5 and 6 are relatively short and the road cyclist, at least, should consider combining them. This would produce a 6hr, 80km ride. For off-road cyclists things are tougher, and even if the difficult legs are avoided 8hr would be needed to get all the way to Plasencia. It would be a shame to rush some wonderful cycling.

The landscape changes on this stage – the *dehesa* has finished for the time being, but a drier, wilder terrain is not much use for arable farming. Livestock farming continues to dominate but with little grass animals are few and far between and the countryside feels empty.

Both the off and on-road routes are just over 50km and involve around 650m of gain and loss. The toughest part of the day is the 200m climb up to pass near Grimaldo.

There are two challenging off-road legs, 5.3.OR and 5.4.OR. The first runs very close to the N-630, and involves a series of short but precipitous climbs and descents, and is very unpleasant. The road alternative involves a lovely empty stretch of road running next to a large and beautiful reservoir. The second challenging leg involves a slog up to the pass near Grimaldo, part of which includes a long steep climb on broken ground. Leg 5.5.OR is also tough, if not quite as challenging; there is a climb at its beginning and the rest is flat but uncomfortable. By opting for the hybrid route, you avoid the two most challenging legs of the off-road route and can reach Grimaldo in about four hours.

On the off-road route there are no refreshment stops after 10km Casar de Cáceres. The road route passes through Cañaveral where there is a bar/

restaurant. Off-road cyclists could make their back to the Cañaveral along the road route at the end of Leg 5 – it's about 2km.

Grimaldo is a small place with just two places to stay. It has a lovely restaurant which should still be open for lunch on arrival.

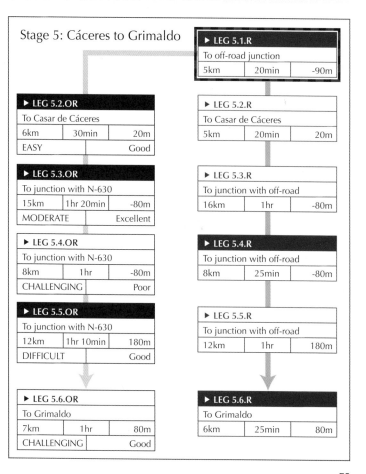

Stage 5: Cáceres to Grimaldo

▶ LEG 5.1.R

To off-road junction

5km	20min	-90m

▶ LEG 5.2.OR

To Casar de Cáceres

6km	30min	20m
EASY		Good

▶ LEG 5.2.R

To Casar de Cáceres

5km	20min	20m

▶ LEG 5.3.OR

To junction with N-630

15km	1hr 20min	-80m
MODERATE		Excellent

▶ LEG 5.3.R

To junction with off-road

16km	1hr	-80m

▶ LEG 5.4.OR

To junction with N-630

8km	1hr	-80m
CHALLENGING		Poor

▶ LEG 5.4.R

To junction with off-road

8km	25min	-80m

▶ LEG 5.5.OR

To junction with N-630

12km	1hr 10min	180m
DIFFICULT		Good

▶ LEG 5.5.R

To junction with off-road

12km	1hr	180m

▶ LEG 5.6.OR

To Grimaldo

7km	1hr	80m
CHALLENGING		Good

▶ LEG 5.6.R

To Grimaldo

6km	25min	80m

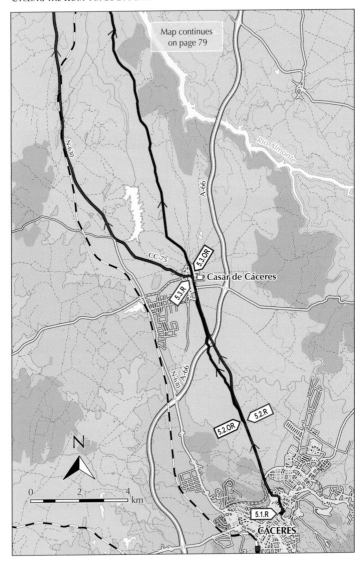

Map continues
on page 79

N-630

Rio Almonte

A-66

CC-75

5.3.OR

5.3.R

Casar de Cáceres

N-630 A-66

5.2.OR

5.2.R

N

0   2   4 km

5.1.R

CÁCERES

ROAD ROUTE

Leg 5.1.R to off-road junction
Take the western exit from the Plaza Mayor heading down the Calle Pintores. Turn right at the Calle Felipe Uribarri and right again into the busier Calle Parras and continue descending in the same direction for about 1km (passing the *churrería* on the way) to traffic lights and a major junction. Cross the N-521, head past the bullring and along to another major junction, this time a roundabout. Crossing the roundabout, take the second exit along a smaller road up a short, steep hill and continue out into the countryside, reaching the junction with the off-road route in about 3km. The road out of Cáceres is small, but busy by Spanish standards, so although it's not far to Casar de Cáceres, the off-road route (where the Camino is rejoined) is worth taking.

Leg 5.2.R to Casar de Cáceres
This leg stays on road and continues, via the interchange with the motorway, into **Casar de Cáceres**. The traffic is better once past the interchange.

Leg 5.3.R to junction with off-road
For the road route, head west from the centre of Casar de Cáceres and join a quiet country road (the CC-75) heading northwest. After 3km join the N-630 and continue for another 13km to the junction with the off-road route.

Leg 5.4.R to junction with off-road
Follow the N-630 close to a large reservoir, the **Embalse de Alcantara,** as it crosses two bridges. On the right are the new elegant bridges built for the high-speed railway. The junction with the off-road route is about 1km past the second bridge.

Stage 5: Road route

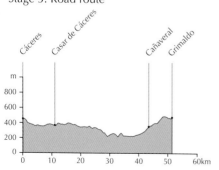

Wild open countryside on the way to Grimaldo

Leg 5.5.R to junction with off-road
Continue along the side of the reservoir for another 4km and start a steady 100m climb up to the small town of **Cañaveral** where refreshments can be found. Continue through the town to a roundabout and the junction with the off-road route.

Leg 5.6.R to Grimaldo
The road route, which continues on the N-630, also crosses the pass, but the climb is a lot easier than the off-road version.

OFF-ROAD (CAMINO) ROUTE

Leg 5.1.R to off-road junction
For the first leg, follow Leg 5.1.R as described in the road route.

Stage 5: Off-road route

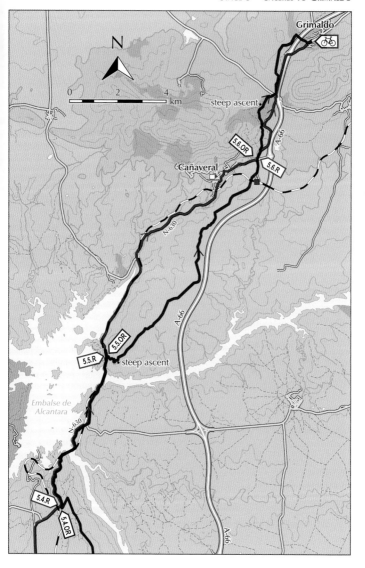

Navigating the numerous gates on the way to Grimaldo

Leg 5.2.OR to Casar de Cáceres

Escaping the busy and narrow road follow an agricultural track north, underneath the motorway, into **Casar de Cáceres**.

> **Casar de Cáceres** is the home of one of Spain's best-loved cheeses, the Torta de Casar. If cheese is your thing, stay at the excellent value Albergue Turistico, Ruta de la Plata de Cesar (tel +34 927 291 193) and eat the cheese at the Majuca restaurant.

Leg 5.3.OR to junction with N-630

Leg 5.3 is the best part of the stage and follows a stone-walled agricultural road north along a ridge. It's a lovely route with great views in all directions.

Continue north through Casar de Cáceres to the edge of town, cross a junction and join a gravel track. On the left is a restored circular building, a Cañada Reale shepherd shelter. Continue north along a walled lane for almost 15km with occasional gates presenting the only diversion along an otherwise perfect route. After 15km the route turns left and heads down towards the N-630. If taking the recommended hybrid option continue to the road, otherwise turn right onto a narrow path. Here the original Camino route has been diverted to make way for a high-speed rail route.

Leg 5.4.OR to junction with N-630

Running parallel to the road, the off-road route follows a narrow footpath ascending and descending a series of steep gullies. It's a difficult route and, with a lovely empty stretch of road cycling just a few yards away, is not worth the effort.

Leg 5.5.OR to junction with N-630

From the junction with N-630 follow a steeply climbing gravel track south and then east (an 80m climb) and then northeast across a dry and fairly barren upland. The track is hard and bumpy and some interesting information boards halfway along suggest that when the Romans maintained it the surface was better. After crossing a first-generation railway line the trail reaches the N-630, follows it for 300m before re-joining the off-road route.

Note: The new railway line was under construction when the author passed through in 2019 and some details of the route may have changed since then.

Leg 5.6.OR to Grimaldo

The final off-road stretch involves a steep climb along a wide gravelly track over a pass. Most people will need to get off their bikes and push for a least 100m of ascent. The final stretch, along a narrow stretch of single track into Grimaldo itself, is also challenging. The recommendation is to take the road route.

For the off-road route leave the N-630 and take a left turn 300m after the roundabout. After 1km of gentle ascent the steep climb up to the pass starts. Continue down from the pass, cross a road and follow an easy path downhill for 3km before turning right and following signs into **Grimaldo**. The last single-track stretch could be avoided by ignoring the turn-off and following the original trail until it reaches a road, turning right onto this road, heading up to the N-630 and then back into Grimaldo.

GRIMALDO

After being over-stimulated at Cáceres and Mérida, a nice quiet evening at Grimaldo, a roadside village with just a few houses, might be just what is needed. Accommodation can be found at the municipal *albergue* (tel +34 645 125 102) or at a *casa rural*, La Posada de Grimaldo, which is more comfortable. You can get a late lunch at the Asador Grimaldo or, catering for pilgrims, a relatively early dinner.

STAGE 6
Grimaldo to Plasencia

Start	Grimaldo
Distance	Road 33km, off-road 42km, hybrid 45km
Ascent	Road 230m, off-road 480m
Descent	Road 350m, off-road 600m
Time	Road 2hr, off-road 3hr 40min, hybrid 2hr 50min
Hybrid route	Same as off-road route

Stage 6 is particularly easy, 33km for the road route and 42km for the off-road route. The off-road route offers excellent cycling through pretty countryside and after Galisteo, a lovely little town with Moorish walls, follows empty country roads. Plasencia is an interesting destination with plenty to see, but even with its attractions a 33km ride along the N-630 could be too short a day, so an alternative 45km road route is proposed which also visits Galisteo. From Galisteo, this alternative road route joins up with Leg 6.2.OR and Leg 6.3.OR of the off-road route; both legs are on tarmacked roads and suitable for road bikes.

On the off-road route the best cycling is on the first leg where, on a gently descending trail, the lovely *dehesa* landscape once again returns. Following a tarmacked country lane after Galisteo the route tracks the River Jerte and is flat, before joining a larger road that climbs steadily to Plasencia.

Plasencia, a founding member of the Ruta Vía de la Plata Association, is not actually on the Camino and as such could be regarded as a detour. If you're only interested in cycling the Camino, stay in the little town of Carcaboso.

ROAD ROUTE

Leg 6.1.R to N-630 turn-off
Follow the N-630 northeast, tracking and sometimes crossing the motorway, and navigating a complex intersection with a second motorway after 23km.

Stage 6: Grimaldo to Plasencia

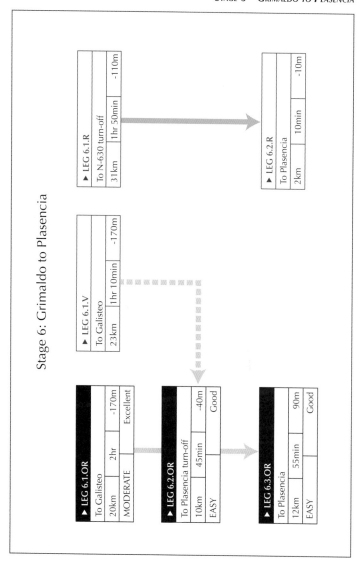

LEG 6.1.OR

To Galisteo

20km	2hr	-170m
MODERATE		Excellent

LEG 6.2.OR

To Plasencia turn-off

10km	45min	-40m
EASY		Good

LEG 6.3.OR

To Plasencia

12km	55min	90m
EASY		Good

LEG 6.1.V

To Galisteo

23km	1hr 10min	-170m

LEG 6.1.R

To N-630 turn-off

31km	1hr 50min	-110m

LEG 6.2.R

To Plasencia

2km	10min	-10m

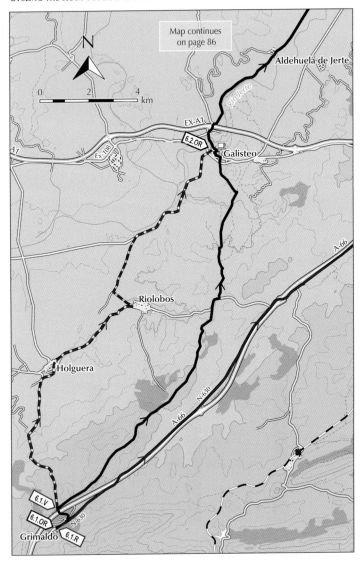

Map continues on page 86

Stage 6: Road route

Leg 6.2.R to Plasencia
After 31km leave the N-630 and follow a road for 2km down to **Plasencia**.

Variant road route

Leg 6.1.V to Galisteo
Head east out of Grimaldo along the N-630 and turn left into a country lane.
Follow this lane to the village of **Holguera** (8km) and continue for another 4km to
Riolobos. On the western edge of the village, take a sharp right turn and without
entering Riolobos continue north to **Galisteo**.

Follow Leg 6.2.OR and Leg 6.3.OR off-road legs along a sealed tarmac surface to **Plasencia**.

OFF-ROAD (CAMINO) ROUTE

Leg 6.1.OR to Galisteo
In the recent past there was a dispute with a landowner which meant the route
was diverted via Riolobos. Happily the argument has been resolved, the original
route restored and the signs which suggest going via Riolobos can be ignored.

Head east out of Grimaldo along the N-630 and turn left into a country lane.
Descend and pass underneath the motorway, turning right after 100m onto a
grassy track. Continue northeast along this track, with occasional stops for gates,
for about 12km (ignoring the turn-off to the Riolobos after about 7km) to another
country road. Turn right and follow the road as it climbs around a corner for 800m
and take a left turn onto an agricultural track. Continue north for 4km, bear left at
a fork near farm buildings and follow a track to a road where the walled town of
Galisteo, with its refreshments, should be visible.

Stage 6: Off-road route

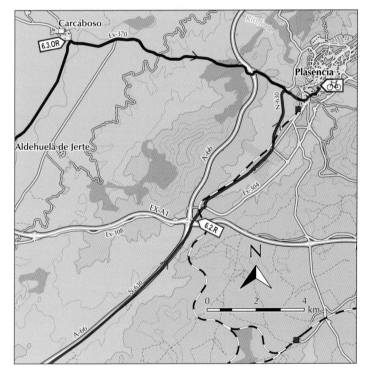

Leg 6.2.OR to Plasencia turn-off

Taking the western gate out of Galisteo follow the road downhill to a beautiful bridge over the **River Jerte**. In spring the towers on the bridge will have storks in residence. Follow the road and turn right at a junction, take the second exit at a roundabout, pass underneath the motorway and take the second exit at the next roundabout. Continue north along a country road through the village of **Aldehuela de Jerte** to a junction and the Plasencia turn-off.

Leg 6.3.OR to Plasencia

Follows a larger but quiet road all the way to Plasencia, climbing nearly 200m before descending into the town and joining up with the road route on the way.

> If you don't want to stay in Plasencia (it's 10km off the RVP) then consider staying at **Carcaboso**. Good value accommodation can be found at the Hostal Ciudad de Cáparra (www.ciudaddecaparra.com), which also has a restaurant.

PLASENCIA

Plasencia is another tightly packed medieval town (pop 41,000) located defensively on a bend in the Jerte River. Its huge intact walls contain an amazing cathedral complex.

Plasencia was a frontier town built in the late 12th century as a defence against the Almohad dynasty. It soon prospered, had the largest Jewish community in Extremadura, and in the 13th century, Christians, Jews and Muslims all lived inside its city walls. In the 15th century the town was home to the first university in Extremadura.

The narrow alleys and streets are ideal for exploring, but any wandering has to end up in the cathedral complex, where two cathedrals side-by-side, provide a case study in the development of architectural styles. The old cathedral was started in 1198, a year after Plasencia was founded, essentially Romanesque but with Gothic elements. As New World money poured into Spain, a more ambitious plan was adopted, some of the old cathedral was knocked down and a new Gothic construction begun, which included Renaissance elements. Both cathedrals are still in use.

If you can get access, it's worth having a good look at the carvings in the choir in the 'new' cathedral. Obscene anti-semitic carvings around the pews reflect growing religious persecution through the 15th century.

There are two top-of-the-range places to stay, both in beautiful buildings. The first is the parador situated in the 15th-century Santo Domingo

The Romanesque cathedral in Plasencia

Monastery, worth visiting even if you are not actually staying there. The second is the Hotel Palacio Carvajal Girón a stunning converted Renaissance palace near the main square. It has more of a boutique style and is none the worse for that.

There is also plenty of mid-priced accommodation, but for a budget option consider the Albergue Santa Ana (https://albergueplasencia.com/).

For food, the reasonably priced Restaurante Succo, just off the main square, is a good option.

STAGE 7

Plasencia to Béjar

Start	Plasencia
Distance	Road 57km, off-road 79km, hybrid 74km
Ascent	Road 1050m, off-road 1230m
Descent	Road 470m, off-road 650m
Time	Road 4hr 5min, off-road 6hr 55min, hybrid 6hr 10min
Hybrid route	Leg 7.1.OR → Leg 7.2.R → Leg 7.3.R → Leg 7.4.R → Leg 7.5.R → Leg 7.6.R.

Stage 7 involves crossing the pass that divides Extramadura from Castile y León and is the highest pass on the route so far. The off-road route in particular is potentially tough and if all legs are completed could involve 7hr in the saddle. The compensation, however, is spectacular cycling, and the 30km leg from Carcaboso through to the N-630 is one of the best on the whole RVP. The route traverses a vast expanse of *dehesa* before emerging into the ruins of the Roman town of Caparra, passing through its famous arch on the way.

The road route is straightforward and much shorter. One of its advantages is that it maximises the amount of time available to visit the town of Hervás, 5km off the route. Its perfectly preserved Jewish quarter, complete with half-timbered houses, is a famous national landmark. Whichever route you are taking, a detour to Hervás for lunch is an attractive proposition.

The hybrid route also shortens the day and makes the cycling easier. One leg is removed because it involves an unnecessary dogleg, and the other because it involves a steep descent from the pass at the end of the day and a long road climb into Béjar.

If all these options seem too much, there are ways to shorten the day. Béjar, at the end of the stage, is not on the Camino and, as with Plasencia, could potentially be missed out. It's an interesting town with a real mountain feel, but there isn't as much to see as in Plasencia and food and accommodation choices are rather limited. A good alternative (avoiding the slight Béjar detour) would be Baños de Montemayor, a spa town reached before crossing the pass.

Stage 7: Plasencia to Béjar

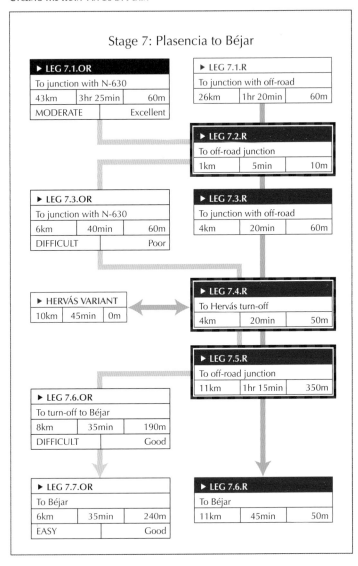

► LEG 7.1.OR

To junction with N-630

43km	3hr 25min	60m
MODERATE		Excellent

► LEG 7.1.R

To junction with off-road

26km	1hr 20min	60m

► LEG 7.2.R

To off-road junction

1km	5min	10m

► LEG 7.3.OR

To junction with N-630

6km	40min	60m
DIFFICULT		Poor

► LEG 7.3.R

To junction with off-road

4km	20min	60m

► HERVÁS VARIANT

10km	45min	0m

► LEG 7.4.R

To Hervás turn-off

4km	20min	50m

► LEG 7.5.R

To off-road junction

11km	1hr 15min	350m

► LEG 7.6.OR

To turn-off to Béjar

8km	35min	190m
DIFFICULT		Good

► LEG 7.7.OR

To Béjar

6km	35min	240m
EASY		Good

► LEG 7.6.R

To Béjar

11km	45min	50m

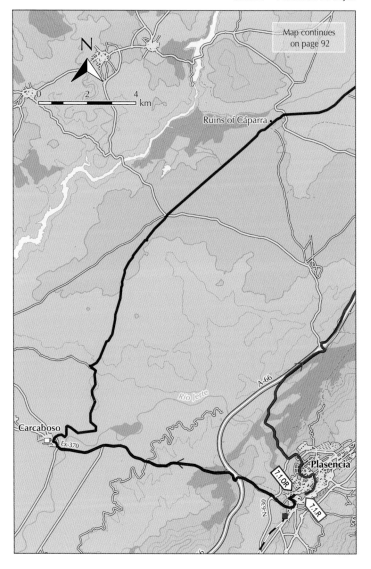

Map continues
on page 92

N

Ruins of Cáparra

Río Jerte

A-66

Carcaboso

EX-370

Plasencia

7.1 OR

7.1 R

N-630

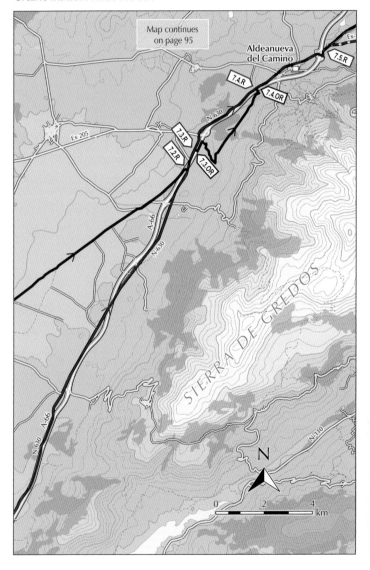

Map continues
on page 95

ROAD ROUTE

Stage 7: Road route

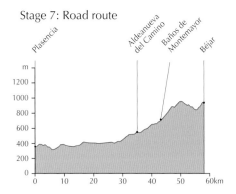

Leg 7.1.R to junction with off-road
Take the northeastern exit from the Plaza Mayor to join the Avenue la Salle and follow it north past the ruins of a convent tower, down towards a park and its medieval aqueduct. Continue west along the Avenue Salamanca to the **N-630**. Follow the N-630 north for another 24km.

Leg 7.2.R to off-road junction
Continue north along the N-630 underneath the motorway and past a junction. If taking the off-road route take the next right onto a service road.

Motorcyclists on the N-630 heading south

Leg 7.3.R to junction with off-road
Continue on the N-630 for 4km to the junction with the off-road.

Leg 7.4.R to Hervás turn-off
Continue on the N-630 for 4km to Hervás turn-off. If not going to Hervás, consider stopping at **Aldeanueva del Camino** for refreshments. It's reached shortly after the road and off-road routes combine. Otherwise continue through the town, over an intersection with the motorway, to the junction with the Hervás turn-off.

Hervás variant
Hervás is 5km away and involves a gentle climb. The N-630 can be picked up again either by retracing your steps or by leaving the town in a more north-westerly direction and rejoining the route further north.

> Located off the main RVP, **Hervás** is a much-visited hill-top town famous for its densely packed historic Jewish quarter, featuring half-timbered houses.

Leg 7.5.R to off-road junction
Follow the N-630 north through **Baños de Montemayor** and up a nicely graded hill, to leave Extremadura and enter Castile y León. From Baños de Montemayor to the top of the pass involves a 200m climb. The Camino itself takes a more direct route, not attempted by the author, but likely to involve a lot of pushing.

> A small spa town nestled underneath the first big hill on the RVP, **Baños de Montemayor** presents a good alternative to Béjar as an end-of-stage destination. The original spa dates back to Roman times, but the modernised version, on the original site, is considered an obligatory stop for those walking the Camino.
>
> Baños de Montemayor has an abundance of hotels – all mid-priced. The Hostal las Termas has particularly good reviews and is close to the spa (www.lastermas.es). For pilgrimage-style accommodation stay at the Albergue Vía de la Plata (tel +34 655 620 515). The Restaurante El Puente, in a lovely location, is the best place to eat, with good vegetarian options.

Leg 7.6.R to Béjar
To avoid some 200m of descent and ascent, take the most direct route to Béjar and stay on the N-630.

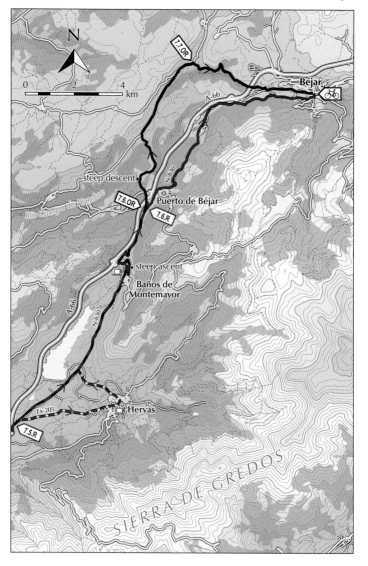

OFF-ROAD (CAMINO) ROUTE

Leg 7.1.OR to junction with N-630

Retrace yesterday's final off-road stage and head down the road to **Carcaboso**. Go north through the town and join a farm track on its northeastern side. Follow the farm track east and then north to some buildings and turn east again. Continue for 1km to a junction and turn left, heading north. As the route continues north the *dehesa* landscape starts to dominate. After another 10km cross a road near a building and now, bearing northeast, continue for another 5km to the ruins of the Roman town of **Cáparra**. After a brief sojourn on a country road to the north of

The ruins of the Roman town of Cáparra

Stage 7: Off-road route

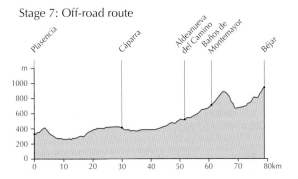

the ruins, rejoin a farm track and continue for another 12km through a more open landscape to the N-630. After passing underneath the motorway turn right (ignoring Camino signs) and up to the N-630.

Leg 7.2.R to off-road junction
Follow the short Leg 7.2.R to the off-road junction, as described in the road route.

Leg 7.3.OR to junction with N-630
The recommendation to avoid this stretch is marginal – it's not difficult – but it is a detour for no particular purpose on what, if the intention is to visit Hervás, is a long day.

Follow the service road north alongside the N-630, turn right after 200m, pass underneath the motorway and turn left and then right after 400m. Continue southeast along a track for 1km before turning sharply left and heading north for 3km. Turn left just beyond some farm buildings and follow a track underneath the motorway and back to the N-630.

Leg 7.4.R to Hervás turn-off
Return to the road and follow Leg 7.4.R as described in the road route.

Leg 7.5.R to off-road junction
Continue on the road route north on Leg 7.5.R as described in the road route.

Leg 7.6.OR to turn-off to Béjar
This leg, with its steep descent, only makes sense if Béjar is being missed.

Sharing the Ruta with Italian cyclists

Leave the N-630 (best to ignore an earlier turning) and continue underneath the motorway (past some Ruta Vía de la Plata information boards provided by Castile y León), over a road and onto a forest track. The route then starts a 200m descent which finishes when it crosses a river and turns right onto a country road. Continue on this road for 4km to a junction with tomorrow's Béjar return leg.

Leg 7.7.OR to Béjar
If not going to Béjar, turn left at this junction (tomorrow's first leg). Otherwise, start a steady 200m climb along a road up to the town.

BÉJAR

Béjar (pop 13,000), with its stone houses and heavy tiled roofs, feels like a mountain town. The old town, positioned on a ridge of rock in the middle of a valley, has the perfect defensive position, although the huge abandoned mills on the riverside below suggest that its best days may be behind it.

Founded in the early 13th century, the town was built originally as a bulwark against Muslim advances. In the 14th and 15th century, Christians, Jews and Muslims co-existed and it hosted a significant Jewish quarter. The town developed an early reputation for textile production which it sustained into the 20th century and until the

Béjar is a town with a mountainous feel

early 1970s was one of Spain's most prosperous industrial towns.

Exploring the old town, including a walk along well-preserved defensive walls, is an excellent pre-dinner activity. Watch out for the Palace of the Duke of Béjar, an austere granite Renaissance building near the main square in the old town.

Well worth a visit is the Jewish Museum David Melul, housed in a 15th-century building next to the Church of St Mary. It includes a brilliant model of the old town detailing how the different religious groups co-existed and describes what happened to the Jews on expulsion; those who stayed and were forcibly converted (the conversos) and those who left Spain.

Béjar is not a major tourist town and, given its size, accommodation options are relatively limited. The best hotel is the Hotel Spa Colón, reasonably priced and in a good location. The town is not directly on the Camino and there is no dedicated pilgrimage accommodation.

For traditional food in either a lively bar or its quieter restaurant, go to Abrasador de Armando near the Palace of the Duke of Béjar.

STAGE 8
Béjar to Salamanca

Start	Béjar
Distance	Road 79km, off-road 81km, hybrid 84km
Ascent	Road 750m, off-road 940m
Descent	Road 890m, off-road 1080m
Time	Road 5hr, off-road /hr, hybrid 6lıı 50min
Hybrid route	Leg 8.1.OR ➜ Leg 8.2.R ➜ Leg 8.3.OR ➜ Variant to Frades de la Sierra ➜ Leg 8.4.R ➜ Leg 8.5.R ➜ Leg 8.6.OR

Stage 8 is another excellent cycling day and, on the off-road, features a lovely stretch of Roman road where the original mile markers are still in place. The wooded *dehesa* of Stage 7 is gradually replaced by a more open landscape typical of the *meseta*.

The road route leaves the N-630 and follows quiet country roads near the off-road route. It's a very pleasant and good option if you want to get to Salamanca in time for lunch.

If the off-road route is taken, there is a significant hill in the middle with a challenging single-track ascent/descent. It is recommended an alternative off-road variant is followed (see Leg 8.4.OR).

There are a number of villages along the route where refreshments can be found both for mid-morning coffee and something more substantial around lunch time.

ROAD ROUTE

Leg 8.1.R to Valverde de Valdelacasa
Turn left out of the Hotel Spa Colón, take an oblique right onto the Paseo Ramón y Cajal and at its end, turn left on to Calle Sanchez Ocana, the main shopping street. Continue west to the Plaza Mayor, cross it and bear right and then right again heading to the castle. Turn right and join the Ronda de Viriata as it swings east and crosses a bridge, before turning right and then sharp left (heading west

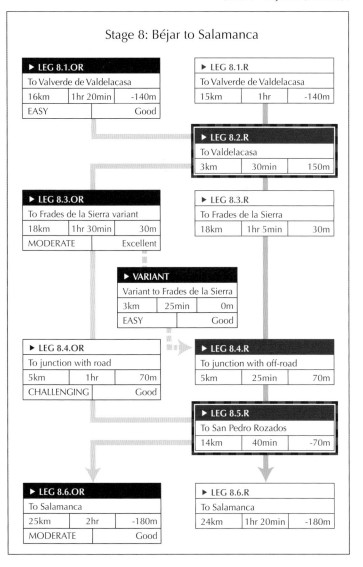

Stage 8: Béjar to Salamanca

► LEG 8.1.OR
To Valverde de Valdelacasa
| 16km | 1hr 20min | -140m |
| EASY | | Good |

► LEG 8.1.R
To Valverde de Valdelacasa
| 15km | 1hr | -140m |

► LEG 8.2.R
To Valdelacasa
| 3km | 30min | 150m |

► LEG 8.3.OR
To Frades de la Sierra variant
| 18km | 1hr 30min | 30m |
| MODERATE | | Excellent |

► LEG 8.3.R
To Frades de la Sierra
| 18km | 1hr 5min | 30m |

► VARIANT
Variant to Frades de la Sierra
| 3km | 25min | 0m |
| EASY | | Good |

► LEG 8.4.OR
To junction with road
| 5km | 1hr | 70m |
| CHALLENGING | | Good |

► LEG 8.4.R
To junction with off-road
| 5km | 25min | 70m |

► LEG 8.5.R
To San Pedro Rozados
| 14km | 40min | -70m |

► LEG 8.6.OR
To Salamanca
| 25km | 2hr | -180m |
| MODERATE | | Good |

► LEG 8.6.R
To Salamanca
| 24km | 1hr 20min | -180m |

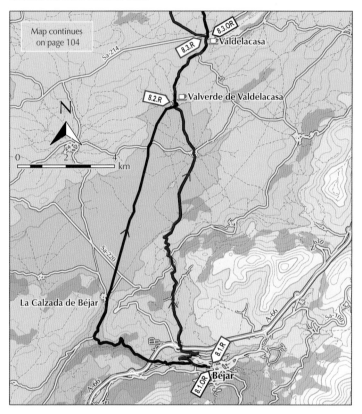

again). After a steep climb, take the first right and head north underneath the motorway, shortly after which the route starts to descend. Follow the signs to **Valverde de Valdelacasa**.

Both Valverde de Valdelacasa and Valdelacasa, the next village, have a bar for a coffee stop.

Leg 8.2.R to Valdelacasa

From Valverde de Valdelacasa follow the quiet road on a steep climb out of the village, north to **Valdelacasa**.

Parked up against a Roman milestone marker

Leg 8.3.R to Frades de la Sierra

Head west out of Valdelacasa, cross the main road, take an oblique right and head northwest. Continue on this road through the villages of **Los Santos** and **Endrinal**, then leave it to turn right into **Frades de la Sierra**.

Leg 8.4.R to junction with off-road

Head east out of Frades de la Sierra, turn left at a junction (the junction with the off-road variant) and head north up and over the Peña de la Huerta. As the road descends and turns east, it reaches the junction with the off-road version.

Leg 8.5.R to San Pedro Rozados

The road and off-road routes combine and continue north along a quiet country road to **San Pedro Rozados** where refreshments are available. The turn-off into San Pedro Rozados is reached after 13km. If you are on the road route and don't want to stop, ignore the turn-off and continue north towards Salamanca.

Stage 8: Road route

103

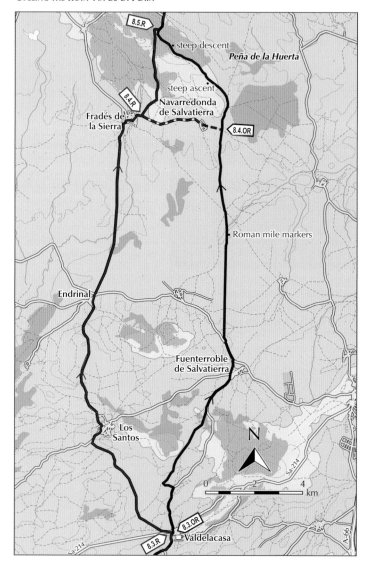

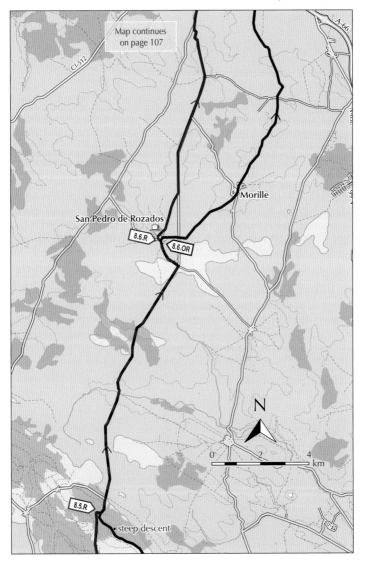

Map continues
on page 107

CL-512

A-66

Morille

San Pedro de Rozados

8.6.R

8.6.OR

N

0   2   4
km

8.5.R

steep descent

Flowers on the meseta on the way to Salamanca

Leg 8.6.R to Salamanca

Take the road heading northeast out of San Pedro Rozados turning left after 2km and right after a further 6km onto a slightly larger road and right again after another 5km. On the southern outskirts of **Salamanca**, take the first exit at a roundabout. After crossing a junction with the N-630 go over the Roman bridge into the city.

OFF-ROAD (CAMINO) ROUTE

Leg 8.1.OR to Valverde de Valdelacasa

From the Hotel Spa Colón in Béjar, head west and turn obliquely left into the Carretera Aldeacipresta. Descend out of the town and follow a road underneath the motorway bridge spanning the valley; then turn right at a junction reached after 6km. Continue to **La Calzada de Béjar**, leaving the road and joining a track just beyond the village. Follow this track to **Valverde de Valdelacasa**.

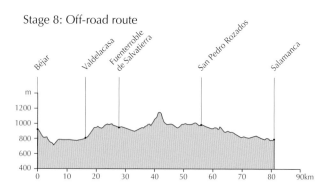
Stage 8: Off-road route

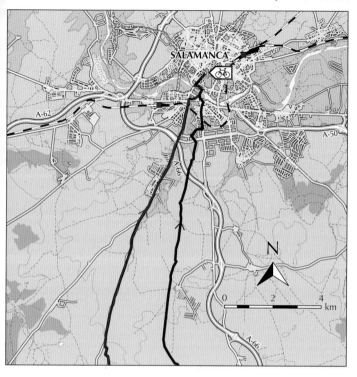

Leg 8.2.R to Valdelacasa
Follow Leg 8.2.R as described in the road route.

Leg 8.3.OR to junction with Frades de la Sierra variant
Crossing the main road running east-west through Valdelacasa join a concrete road to the left of a building and follow it north. Turn sharp left at a junction 1km to the north of the village and follow a dirt road towards a quarry. Continue on the dirt road as it swings northeast for 5km, then turn left onto a road and follow it to **Fuenterroble de Salvatierra**. Pass the village on its western side, turn right after 1km heading into open countryside and a Roman road now covered in grass. Following Roman mile markers continue north for 9km to a gate and a junction with a track running east-west.

Leg 8.4.OR to junction with road

This challenging leg involves climbing over a small mountain, the wind turbine-festooned Peña de la Huerta.

Continue north for 1km and then turn left onto an increasingly difficult path ascending steeply through scrub. The descent is even more precipitous.

Variant to Frades de la Sierra

To avoid Leg 8.4.OR, turn left beyond the gate (at the end of Leg 8.3.OR) and follow the track for 1km to the small settlement of **Navarredonda de Salvetierra**. Take the road on its eastern side and head to **Frades de la Sierra** and join Leg 8.4.R

Leg 8.5.R to San Pedro Rozados

Follow Leg 8.5.R as described in the road route.

Leg 8.6.OR to Salamanca

Join a dirt track heading directly east out of San Pedro Rozados, cross the road onto another dirt track and bear left at a junction 100m later. Head northeast to the village of **Morille** and, on an easy, gently descending route continue all the way to **Salamanca**. Try to enter the city via the Roman bridge.

SALAMANCA

Salamanca (pop 150,000) is a buzzing university city, the old centre of which is packed with monumental buildings. The buildings are constructed using a distinct blond sandstone. At sunset its 'golden city' designation is easily understood.

The city's origins are Celtic, possibly even pre-Celtic. It was fought over by Hannibal and, with the eventual fall of the Carthagians, occupied by the Romans who built the bridge in the 1st century. A bishopric in the time of the Visigoths, it was on the front line for several centuries and during the Muslim domination of Spain became depopulated. The definitive Christian resettlement took place in the late 11th century.

When Alfonso IX of León granted its university a royal charter in 1218, Salamanca became one of the most significant and prestigious academic centres in Europe. In the 16th century the city had a population of 24,000 including 6,000 students.

The old city centre is another UNESCO World Heritage Site and the award is based on its combination of religious and university buildings and its open spaces. For a city sampler, head to the heart of the old city, the

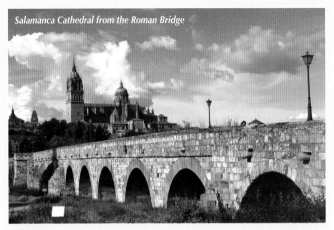

Salamanca Cathedral from the Roman Bridge

Baroque-style Plaza Mayor, and from there take a short walk to either the 15th-century fortress tower of Clavero or the Palace of Monterrey and its amazing Renaissance interiors. Walk south towards the cathedral, passing the Casa de las Conchas, a Gothic palace covered in scallop shells from the Camino. The huge cathedral with its 92m bell tower is unmissable. Like Plasencia, Salamanca has two connected cathedrals. The newer Gothic one dominates from the outside and features both Gothic and Baroque elements (it wasn't finished until the 18th century). Finish the tour with a change of scale and pop into the Casa Lis a Art Nouveau, a famous Art Déco museum near the cathedral.

Accommodation in the city centre is more expensive (the parador is a modern building outside the city centre) but if you can afford it, consider the Palacio de Castellanos, in a beautifully restored building near the cathedral, or nearby, the Hospes Palacio de San Esteban. The Hostal Plaza Mayor is good value, but be warned that some of the rooms can be noisy. For pilgrimage-style accommodation try the municipal *albergue*, the Casa la Calera (tel +34 652 921 185).

There are lots of places to eat. Consider the Restaurante La Hoja 21 which serves modern Spanish food, excellent but relatively pricey. Also very good, and cheaper, are the Tapas 2.0 Gastrotasca, along with the less trendy Tapas 3.0 located just around the block.

STAGE 9
Salamanca to Zamora

Start	Salamanca
Distance	Road 68km, off-road 70km, hybrid 69km
Ascent	Road 420m, off-road 580m
Descent	Road 420m, off-road 580m
Time	Road 3hr 35min, off-road 5hr 40min, hybrid 4hr 40min
Hybrid route	Leg 9.1.R ➜ Leg 9.2.OR ➜ Leg 9.3.R ➜ Leg 9.4.OR

Stage 9 offers a shorter day and getting to Zamora in time for lunch is possible whichever option is chosen. There are no significant climbs and it should take just under four hours to complete the road route and well under five hours to finish the hybrid route.

In this and the following stage, parts of the original Camino have been messed up by motorway construction, particularly on the central off-road leg (9.3.OR), so taking the road leg (9.3.R) on an empty N-630 is recommended instead. Fortunately, the off-road route does improve and the final leg, involving a gentle cross-country descent to Zamora, is very good.

The landscape is open and similar to that experienced on the approach to Salamanca.

ROAD ROUTE

Leg 9.1.R to Aldeaseca de Armuña
From the Roman bridge, head west along the northern bank of the river, join the **N-630** and follow it north out of the city, underneath the motorway and out into countryside. The Camino is running alongside the road on this stretch. Arrive at **Aldeaseca de Armuña**, where the off-road route leaves the N-630.

Leg 9.2.R to junction with off-road
Continue north along the N-630. For a break, consider one of several bars/restaurants on the edge of **Calzada de Valdunciel**, 16km north of Salamanca.

Stage 9: Road route

Stage 9: Salamanca to Zamora

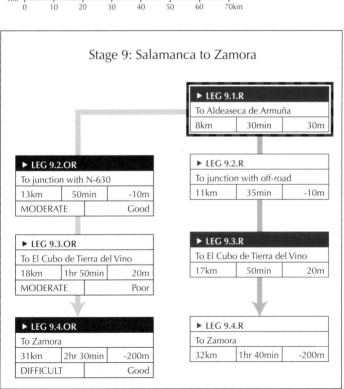

▶ LEG 9.1.R		
To Aldeaseca de Armuña		
8km	30min	30m

▶ LEG 9.2.OR		
To junction with N-630		
13km	50min	-10m
MODERATE		Good

▶ LEG 9.2.R		
To junction with off-road		
11km	35min	-10m

▶ LEG 9.3.OR		
To El Cubo de Tierra del Vino		
18km	1hr 50min	20m
MODERATE		Poor

▶ LEG 9.3.R		
To El Cubo de Tierra del Vino		
17km	50min	20m

▶ LEG 9.4.OR		
To Zamora		
31km	2hr 30min	-200m
DIFFICULT		Good

▶ LEG 9.4.R		
To Zamora		
32km	1hr 40min	-200m

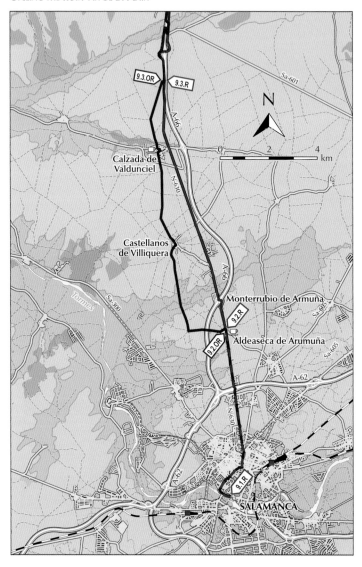

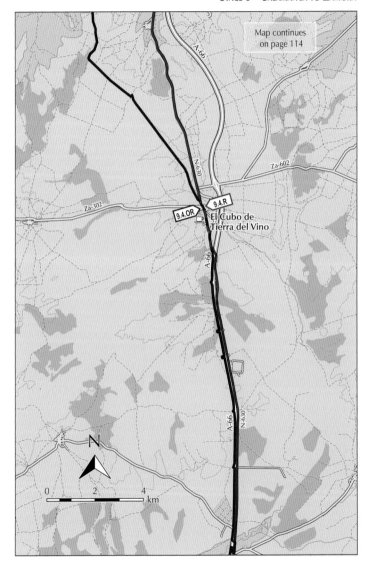

Map continues
on page 114

A-66

A-66

N-630

Za-602

Za-302

9.4.R

9.4.OR

El Cubo de
Tierra del Vino

A-66

A-66

N-630

N

0   2   4
km

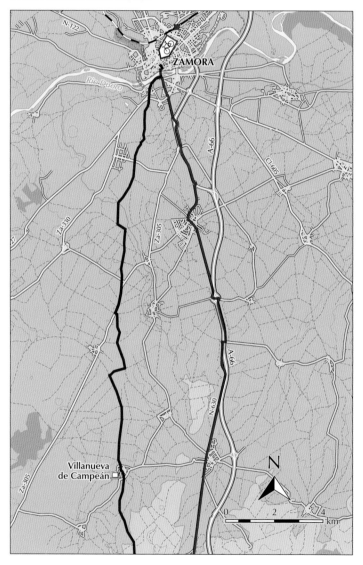

Heading into Zamora

Leg 9.3.R to El Cubo de Tierra del Vino
Continue north along the N-630, leaving it after 16km to head into **El Cubo de Tierra del Vino** where there is a bar for refreshments.

Leg 9.4.R to Zamora
Rejoin the N-630 just to the north of El Cubo de Tierra del Vino, enjoying a steady descent after 5km. Leave the N-630 after 30km at a junction to the south of the **Zamora** and head directly into the city.

OFF-ROAD (CAMINO) ROUTE

Leg 9.1.R to Aldeaseca de Armuña
Follow Leg 9.1R to **Aldeaseca de Armuña** – see description under road route.

Leg 9.2.OR to junction with N-630
Join a dirt track to the west of Aldeaseca de Armuña, follow it underneath the motorway and take a sharp right at a junction 800m later. Continue north along an agricultural road to **Castellanos de Villiquera**, go through the village and, after crossing a road on its northwestern side, head north into the countryside along another agricultural road to **Calzada de Valdunciel**. Go through the town past the town hall and over a road on its northern side heading, once more, into the countryside. Bear right at a junction 1km later and continue to the **N-630**.

Off-road on the way to Zamora

Leg 9.3.OR to El Cubo de Tierra del Vino
The off-road route runs alongside the N-630 before switching its allegiance to the motorway. It's an unattractive stretch of gravel track built for the pilgrims and only worth doing if you hate cycling along an empty N-630.

Leg 9.4.OR to Zamora
Continue north out of **El Cubo de Tierra del Vino**, turning left onto a dirt road 100m from the edge of the village. After following the route of an abandoned railway line for 4km turn left and join a descending agricultural road to the village of **Villanueva de Campeán**. Pass through the village, continue north on another agricultural road for 4km and turn right to climb up to a road. Follow the road north for about 300m, turn left onto a dirt track and go north into the southern outskirts of **Zamora**. Cross the first bridge you come to over the **Río Duoro** and go up a road to the heart of the city.

Stage 9: Off-road route

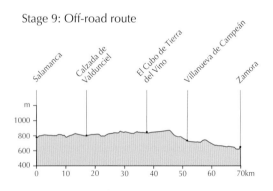

ZAMORA

Zamora (pop 65,000) is a gem of a place. It sits above the Duoro river and its Muslim city walls contains the world's greatest concentration of Romanesque churches.

A settlement existed here before the Romans arrived, but the city probably got its name from the Visigoths who called it Semure. It was on the Muslim/Christian front line and changed hands a number of times between the 8th and 10th centuries, becoming heavily fortified as a result. When finally captured by the Christians, its strategic position on the Duoro and the commercial value of its water mills generated huge wealth and financed the building of the cathedral and numerous Romanesque churches. Some 24 churches still survive, although the number was originally larger.

There is a lot to see, but because everything is in a small area it's possible to take it in quickly.

A good place to get your bearings is the Plaza Mayor, which features bars, cafés and the Church of San Juan. From here, go southwest into a square with government buildings and the parador – located in the lovely 15th-century Palacio de los Condes de Alba y Aliste. Continue southwest passing Santa María Magdalena, another Romanesque church and shortly

Zamora has the world's biggest concentration of Romanesque churches

after bear left passing the Iglesia de San Idelfonso and enter a small square featuring the Convento Religiosas Marinas. Continue west and turn left at the Tourist Information Office emerging onto the city wall with views of the Duoro and the medieval bridge, the Puente de Piedra. Continue west through the old city gate and up to the cathedral. The main entrance, Puerta del Obispo, is a combination of Romanesque and Mozarabic. Look out for the

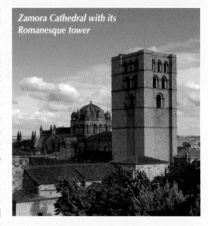

Zamora Cathedral with its Romanesque tower

cathedral's intricate Byzantine dome and classic Romanesque tower. From the cathedral continue on to the castle which, until recently, was largely covered in soil and debris. The views from the castle tower back to the cathedral are excellent. Finally it's worth visiting those financially lucrative medieval water mills, just below the city walls near the castle. There are plenty of places to stay in Zamora. The parador is the upmarket choice, although the cheaper Zamora Palacio del Duero also features an amazing building, but has a modern boutique feel. More contemporary, is the apartment-style San Gil Plaza hotel. For pilgrimage-style accommodation, combining a good location with a restored historic building, go to the Albergue de Peregrinos (tel +34 980 50 94 27).

There is a good choice of restaurants, but the author can offer first-hand recommendation for Los Caprichos de Meneses, just behind the church in the Plaza Mayor. It includes a fine dining restaurant with a bar/tapas alternative at the front.

STAGE 10
Zamora to Benavente

Start	Zamora
Distance	Road 66km, off-road 68km, hybrid 66km
Ascent	Road 450m, off-road 500m
Descent	Road 350m, off-road 400m
Time	Road 3hr 50min, off-road 5hr, hybrid 4hr 15min
Hybrid route	Leg 10.1.OR → Leg 10.2.R → Leg 10.3.R → Leg 10.4.R → Leg 10.5.OR

This is where the route heading north up to Gijón and the Camino Sanabrés going west to Santiago de Compostela split. On the way up to the split, at Granja de Moreruela, the original Camino route has been messed up by both the motorway and the new high-speed railway (the full extent of these changes are not marked on the map). Things start to improve after the split, particularly on the off-road run into Benavente which follows a new cycleway along a disused railway line. For road cyclists, the N-630 remains as reliable as ever, and the hybrid route reverts to the N-630 for two legs.

There are no significant climbs and as there are limited refreshment stops at Montamarta and Granja de Moreruela, it makes sense to plan for lunch in Benavente.

ROAD ROUTE

Leg 10.1.R to Montamarta
Take the northeast exit from the Plaza Mayor and follow the one-way system down to a roundabout, join the **N-630** and follow it to **Montamarta**.

Leg 10.2.R to Granja de Moreruela
Continue north on the N-630, crossing the motorway twice, to **Granja de Moreruela**, which has bars for refreshments.

For cyclists on the Camino Sanabrés, this is where the route leaves the RVP – see Leg 1.1.R of the Camino Sanabrés to continue.

Stage 10: Zamora to Benavente

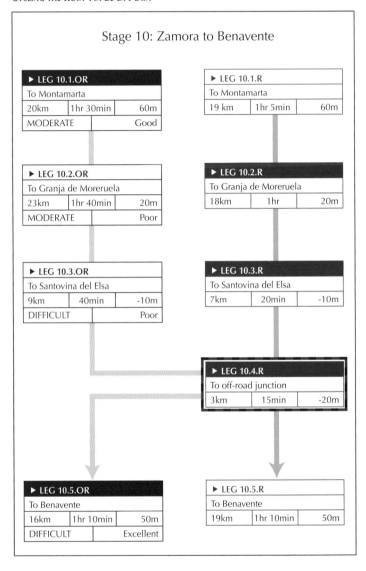

► LEG 10.1.OR		
To Montamarta		
20km	1hr 30min	60m
MODERATE		Good

► LEG 10.1.R		
To Montamarta		
19 km	1hr 5min	60m

► LEG 10.2.OR		
To Granja de Moreruela		
23km	1hr 40min	20m
MODERATE		Poor

► LEG 10.2.R		
To Granja de Moreruela		
18km	1hr	20m

► LEG 10.3.OR		
To Santovina del Elsa		
9km	40min	-10m
DIFFICULT		Poor

► LEG 10.3.R		
To Santovina del Elsa		
7km	20min	-10m

► LEG 10.4.R		
To off-road junction		
3km	15min	-20m

► LEG 10.5.OR		
To Benavente		
16km	1hr 10min	50m
DIFFICULT		Excellent

► LEG 10.5.R		
To Benavente		
19km	1hr 10min	50m

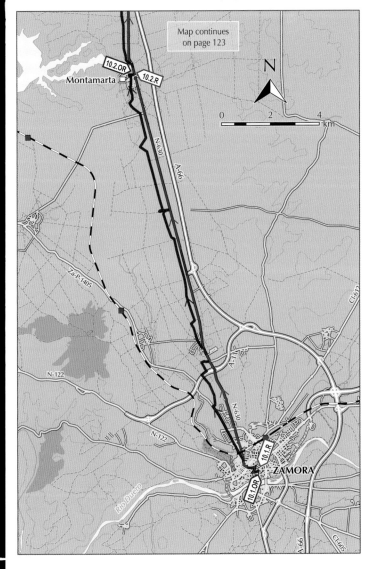

Map continues
on page 123

10.2.OR

10.2.R

Montamarta

N

0   2   4
km

N-630

A-66

Za-P-1405

N-122

A-11

N-630

N-122

CL-612

10.1.R

10.1.OR

ZAMORA

Río Duero

A-66

CL-605

Stage 10: Road route

Leg 10.3.R to Santovina del Elsa
Continue north on the N-630 to **Santovina del Elsa**, which has bars for refreshments.

Leg 10.4.R to off-road junction
Continue for 3km up the N-630 to a roundabout.

Leg 10.5.R to Benavente
From the roundabout, continue north along the N-630. After 11km the route reaches an intersection with a motorway. Cross it and, at the second roundabout on its northern side, take the second exit and follow a small road down to a bridge. Cross the bridge, follow the road under the motorway, continue west for 800m and take a sharp right joining a main road heading into **Benavente**.

OFF-ROAD (CAMINO) ROUTE

Leg 10.1.OR to Montamarta
Take the northeast exit from the Plaza Mayor and follow the one-way system down to a roundabout. Join the N-122, go up a hill for 200m and take an oblique left turn into the Calle de la Hiniesta. Continue for 3km, turn right onto an agricultural road and after passing under a motorway take a sharp right. Turn left after 100m, then right,

The parting of the Caminos

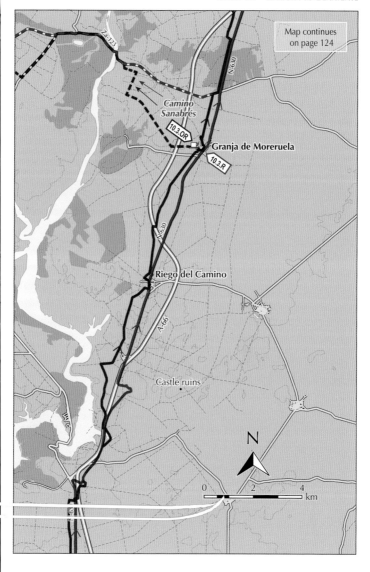

Map continues
on page 124

ZA-123

N-630

*Camino
Sanabrés*

10.3.OR

Granja de Moreruela

10.3.R

N-630

Riego del Camino

A-66

Castle ruins

N

0   2   4
km

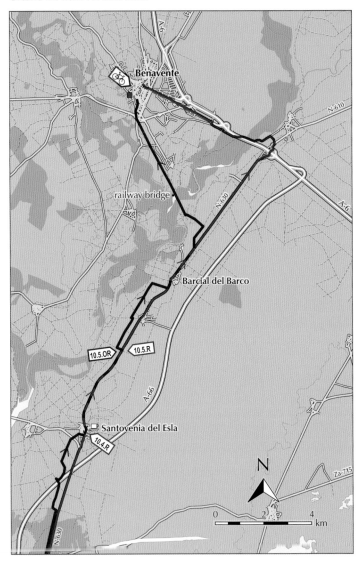

Stage 10: Off-road route

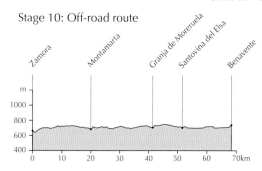

then left again reaching a roundabout and the N-630. Follow an agricultural road that tracks the N-630 all the way to **Montamarta**.

Leg 10.2.OR to Granja de Moreruela

Leg 10.2 is not difficult, but it is ugly and, with long stretches of gravel track running immediately next to either the N-630 or the new motorway, the road route is recommended.

For off-road, cross the bridge from Montamarta, turn left onto a dirt track and follow it climbing north away from the reservoir. Continue for 4km before turning abruptly east (some re-routing here) and cross the motorway via a bridge. Continue north on a gravel track around a complex intersection before crossing the motorway again. After passing the ruins of a castle (the Pilares de Castro) continue north to the village of **Riego del Camino** and on to **Granja de Moreruela**.

> **For cyclists on the Camino Sanabrés, this is where the route leaves the RVP – see Leg 1.1.OR of the Camino Sanabrés to continue.**

Leg 10.3.OR to Santovina del Elsa

The messy off-road cycling continues for another 9km along a more challenging route. Finding what is a steep route out of Granja de Moreruela is the first challenge.

Turn left off N-630 at the junction opposite the town hall, take the first right and second left and follow a road climbing up through the village. At the top of the hill turn sharp right, then left, and follow a track into the countryside for 2km to a road. Turn right and then left at a roundabout and follow a track running next to the N-630. Eventually the track veers away from the N-630, crosses the motorway and continues north to **Santovina del Elsa**.

Leg 10.4.R to off-road junction
Join the N-630 and follow Leg 10.4.R as described in the road route.

Leg 10.5.OR to Benavente
Take the third exit from the roundabout onto an agricultural track and turn right after 200m. Go north for 3km, turn right and join the N-630 as it passes through the village of **Barcial de Barco** before leaving it to join a dirt track on the right immediately north of the village. After passing underneath the N-630, continue for 1km and take a sharp left. After a further 1km join an old railway line, crossing a river on the original railway bridge, and follow it to **Benavente**. This is a new cycleway and its further development could affect routing around Barcial de Barco.

BENAVENTE

Benavente (pop 18,000) sits on top of a hill overlooking a vast wooded plain. Although the site was occupied before the reconquest, most of the town's important buildings were constructed after the 12th century.

A good place to start a tour is the parador and the Torre del Caracol. It is the last remaining part of a 12th century palace (the rest was destroyed by Napoleon's army which devastated the city) situated at the end of a ridge. From here, go along the city wall into town to the Romanesque Santa María de Azogue church. Take the first of three easterly exits and go to the

Parked up at the parador in Benavente

Plaza Mayor, a square surrounded by Renaissance buildings. The city's other important Romanesque church, San Juan del Mercado, can be found to the north of the square.

The parador is the best place to stay if you can afford it but, the La Trapería Pensión, located nearby, is a nice and cheaper alternative. For pilgrimage-style accommodation try the Albergue Municipal de Peregrinos (tel +34 980 63 42 11).

For food, the Taberna de Bode is good value and full of locals.

STAGE 11

Benavente to León

Start	Benavente
Distance	Road 102km, off-road 102km, hybrid 102km
Ascent	Road 450m, off-road 500m
Descent	Road 350m, off-road 400m
Time	Road 6hr 5min, off-road 7hr 20min, hybrid 7hr 20min
Hybrid route	Same as off-road route

Stage 11 takes an indirect route to León. It heads northwest, sticking with the original Roman RVP, to La Beñeza, at about two-thirds of the stage, and then turns north to join the Camino Francés (the main Camino route to Santiago de Compostela) and follows it, against the flow of pilgrims, into León. The original Roman road continues northwest from La Beñeza to Astorga which is also on the Camino Francés. Continuing to Astorga from La Beñeza, joining the Camino Francés and heading west is therefore an alternative way of getting to Santiago de Compostela.

Road cyclists who have grown particularly fond of the N-630 should note that the La Beñeza dogleg takes them away from their old friend. It is still there and returning to the N-630 from Benavente and blasting north across a flat plain is the quickest way (30km shorter) to León for those short of time.

At more than 100km, Stage 11 is the longest stage on the whole of the RVP by some margin. The good news is that the route is easy and the height gained is barely noticeable. The bad news is that the final run-in to León, 32km along a relatively busy N-120, is unpleasant. Road cyclists can shelter on the hard shoulder while off-roaders can follow an equally tedious but slower gravel track a couple of metres away.

The rest of the stage, across a fertile agricultural plain, is interesting and has plenty to see. Given a cycling time of over 6hr whichever route you choose, a lunch stop will be required in one of the many little towns en route.

Stage 11: Benavente to León

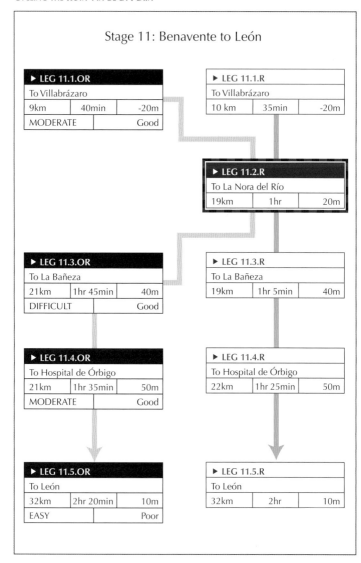

▶ LEG 11.1.OR

To Villabrázaro

9km	40min	-20m
MODERATE		Good

▶ LEG 11.1.R

To Villabrázaro

10 km	35min	-20m

▶ LEG 11.2.R

To La Nora del Río

19km	1hr	20m

▶ LEG 11.3.OR

To La Bañeza

21km	1hr 45min	40m
DIFFICULT		Good

▶ LEG 11.3.R

To La Bañeza

19km	1hr 5min	40m

▶ LEG 11.4.OR

To Hospital de Órbigo

21km	1hr 35min	50m
MODERATE		Good

▶ LEG 11.4.R

To Hospital de Órbigo

22km	1hr 25min	50m

▶ LEG 11.5.OR

To León

32km	2hr 20min	10m
EASY		Poor

▶ LEG 11.5.R

To León

32km	2hr	10m

ROAD ROUTE

Leg 11.1.R to Villabrázaro

Go directly north from the parador, across the small park and through the town via its one-way system, to a large roundabout. Take the third exit and follow a quiet country road into the countryside. After 4km take a right turn and go under the motorway into **Villabrázaro**.

Leg 11.2.R to La Nora del Río

Take the road north out of Villabrázaro for 12km to where it turns left, crosses a lovely **medieval bridge** with an uncomfortable cobbled surface and joins a slightly larger road going west. Follow the road, turning north after 2km into **Alija del Infantado** (a refreshment stop) and through to **La Nora del Río** where the routes diverge.

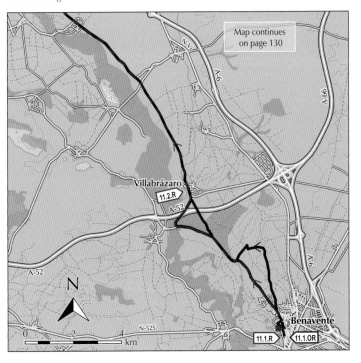

Map continues on page 130

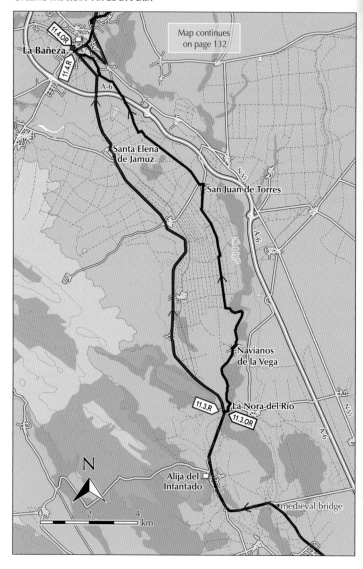

Traditional wine stores beside the route

Leg 11.3.R to La Bañeza

Continue past the turn-off to La Nora del Río going north through a series of small villages to **Santa Elena de Jamuz**. The strange little kiln-like buildings beside the route are traditional wine stores. At Santa Elena de Jamuz turn right at the junction and continue into **La Bañeza**.

Leg 11.4.R to Hospital de Órbigo

The road route goes north just east of the Río Órbigo and is just as quiet as the off-road route. It provides the opportunity to eat river trout in a great restaurant dedicated to this local speciality. For some reason the official route turns east just before reaching Hospital de Órbigo and it's worth carrying on a little just to see the wonderful bridge in its centre.

Stage 11: Road route

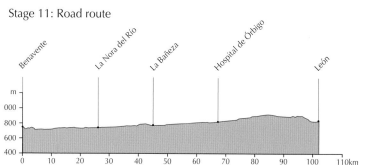

131

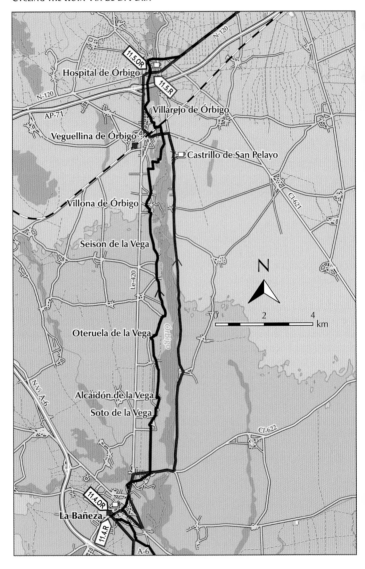

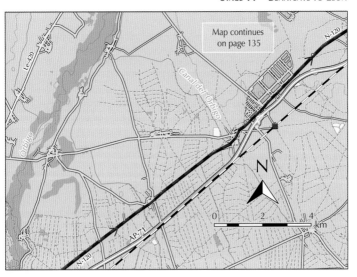

Continue through the centre of La Bañeza (walking where necessary) to a large roundabout, cross it and turn right after 400m. Head east for 1.5km and take the first left, after crossing a bridge, to join a quiet country road. Follow this through a series of small villages for 13km to **Castrillo de San Pelayo** where the Restuarante Natal serves all things trout. Turn left at the junction and go into **Veguellina de Órbigo**. Turn right into the centre of town, and go north to **Hospital de Órbigo**.

Leg 11.5.R to León

From the centre of Hospital de Órbigo turn right and cross the wonderful Roman bridge, the Puente del Paso Honroso. It was the location for a famous medieval joust and a re-enactment now takes place every year on the first weekend in June.

From the bridge, continue east for 200m and take a left turn down to the **N-120**. Road cyclists can slot themselves onto the hard shoulder and follow it all the way to León, whereas off-road cyclists can join the pilgrims' trail which sticks close to the N-120, occasionally switching sides. Both routes have little to commend them. Continue for 26km with the N-120, through a series of small towns and villages, leaving it on the outskirts of **León** as it turns south, and using the underpass, continue along a busy road into the city.

OFF-ROAD (CAMINO) ROUTE

Leg 11.1.OR to Villabrázaro
Go directly north from the parador, across the small park and through the town via its one-way system, to a large roundabout. Take the second exit and, after about 200m as the road swings east, join a dirt track and follow it north for 2km. Turn left, go west for about 1.5km and turn right onto a road. Turn right off the road after 1.5km and follow a dirt track over a small hill and under the motorway into **Villabrázaro**.

Leg 11.2.R to La Nora del Río
Follow Leg 11.2.R as described in the road route.

Leg 11.3.OR to La Bañeza
The off-road route follows agricultural roads through an intensively farmed, flat landscape. The route isn't difficult but can be waterlogged and rutted in places.

Turn right at the junction, follow the road north round the small village of **La Nora del Río**, turn left onto an agricultural road and head north on the left bank of a river through the village of **Navianos de la Vega**. Join a dirt road just to the north of the village and continue with the river as it swings west then north. The route can be overgrown at this point. Join an agricultural road heading directly north to the village of **San Juan de Torres** just beyond the point where the river itself turns north. Join the road going through the village and turn left at the main junction and then right onto an agricultural track after about 200m. Follow this for 3km then join another track into **La Bañeza**.

Stage 11: Off-road route

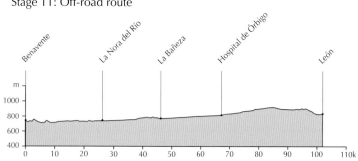

Poppies in a field of wheat

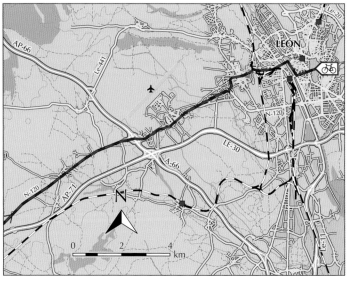

Leg 11.4.OR to Hospital de Órbigo

La Beñeza is a busy little town and it may be easier to get off and walk rather than attempt to cycle through its complicated one-way system.

Follow the main shopping street into the centre of town, past the church, to a large roundabout on the eastern side. Go around the roundabout and join a cycleway. Follow it underneath the main road, across a little park, over an old railway bridge and back across the main road. Continue through a suburb then cross the main road to join a smaller road. Follow this to **Soto de la Vega**. Continue north into **Alcaidón de la Vega**, turn left and then right onto an agricultural track and follow this for 1km to **Oteruela de la Vega**.

Bear right, join a small road and go north through two little villages to **Seison de la Vega**. On its northern side join an agricultural track and follow it to Villoria de Órbigo. Go through the village and take a quiet country road, joining an agricultural track after 1km. Follow this track back to the river and continue north along the riverbank, past a campsite, under a railway line and on to the village of **Veguellina de Órbigo**. Continue north out of the village and into **Hospital de Órbigo**.

Leg 11.5.R to León

Follow 11.5.R as described in the road route, joining the gravel track which sticks close to the N-120, occasionally switching sides.

LEÓN

León (pop 128,000) is my favourite city on the RVP. It boasts amazing historic buildings but has a modern, youthful feel. The cathedral, once inside, is breath-taking.

León was founded as a Roman camp in the final stages of the Carthaginian war and its huge Roman walls are still there near the cathedral. Occupation was sustained by the Visigoths and, building more walls, the Muslims made it the key to their northern defensive line. It was finally taken by the Christians in the 10th century. It became the capital city of the Kingdom of León and enjoyed a golden period for two centuries going into relative decline when the Kingdoms of León and Castille merged and Burgos grabbed its capital spot. The discovery of coal in the 19th century and the construction of a railway line, taking the coal to the steelmills at Bilbao led to a revival, and today the city feels like a prosperous place.

There is a lot to see, but visiting the cathedral when the sun is low is a real highlight.

Consider starting a tour at the Convento de San Marcos, the recently restored parador featuring a dramatic plateresque façade overlooking a

Casa Botines, a Gaudi treasure in León

formal square. Walk east across a roundabout and continue along the street until eventually you reach the huge western walls of the original Roman city. Just around the corner is the Basílica de San Isidoro. This houses a small museum whose prize possession is the Chalice of Doña Urraca, which some claim is the Holy Grail, and the Royal Panteon. The Royal Panteon, a passageway whose arches are decorated with murals, is known as the Sistine Chapel of Romanesque Art. Walk south and take in the Casa Botines, one of only two Gaudí buildings outside Barcelona, and the Palacio De Los Guzmanes, a beautiful Renaissance palace.

Now go to the cathedral which, with 1800m of stained glass, is designed with the sun in mind and best visited in what photographers call the 'golden hours' – just after sunrise and before sunset. Built on – for once – dodgy Roman foundations, its construction and subsequent renovation in the 18th century are both epic tales. Its huge stained-glass windows are enabled by the delicate rib cage form of a vaulted ceiling – the technological breakthrough that enabled Gothic design to succeed Romanesque.By now you'll probably need a drink, so head south into Barrio Húmedo, the 'wet district' famous for its bars, cafés and tapas. The Plaza Mayor is located just east of the wet district and is similar in form to its cousin in Salamanca.

Staying at the parador would be an excellent choice if you can afford it – it is popular with pilgrims on the St James Way. But León does have a huge range of alternatives. For pilgrimage-style accommodation, consider the municipal *albergue* (tel +34 987 081 832).

Like so many Spanish cities, León claims to have the best tapas, and it's great fun exploring the Barrio Húmedo to test the boast. If you need a target, try El Rebote or, for something a little more substantial than a croqueta, El Besugo.

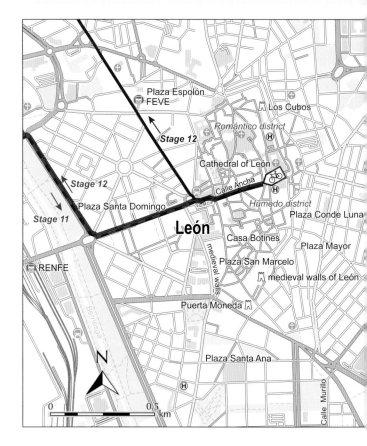

STAGE 12

León to Pola de Lena

Start	León
Distance	Road 84km, off-road 95km, hybrid 94km
Ascent	Road 960m, off-road 2140m
Descent	Road 1500m, off-road 2680m
Time	Road 5hr, off-road 8hr 30min, hybrid 7hr 30min
Hybrid route	Leg 12.1.OR → Leg 12.2.OR → Leg 12.3.R → Leg 12.4.R → Leg 12.5.OR

Stage 12 crosses the Cantabrian mountains. As well as reaching the highest point on the route, it transits from the dry Mediterranean climate to a much damper one dominated by the Atlantic Ocean. Both the road and off-road routes are wonderful, and the final stretch of off-road cycling is really special.

The Stage 12 road route is excellent. The climb to the main pass, the Puerto de Parajes, is steady and following a lovely valley, altitude is gained easily. The descent on the other hand, around a series of hairpin bends, has an alpine quality and is 'exciting'. There are a few short tunnels to contend with, all illuminated, and some slow-moving lorries to watch out for on the descent from the pass. If the weather is bad the descent could be treacherous.

For once the hybrid route includes a stretch of cycling rated as challenging. It's recommended because it's so good. After a tough climb to the pass, the route follows a Roman road along a ridge for 17km. The views are wonderful. The ridge itself is not difficult, following an undulating track wide enough to accommodate farm vehicles. The descent, however, is steep and prolonged and it is this that puts the leg into the challenging category. Good brakes are essential.

The off-road route will take at least 7hr 30min. Avoiding Leg 3 and sticking instead with the N-630 makes it manageable. Leg 3 includes a steep pass, with a climb that involves a lot of pushing, and a precipitous descent.

For an early morning coffee stop at La Robla and for something more substantial before the pass, stop at Villamanin.

Stage 12: León to Pola de Lena

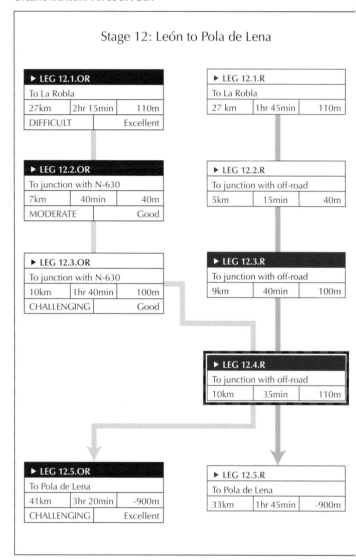

▶ LEG 12.1.OR

To La Robla		
27km	2hr 15min	110m
DIFFICULT		Excellent

▶ LEG 12.1.R

To La Robla		
27 km	1hr 45min	110m

▶ LEG 12.2.OR

To junction with N-630		
7km	40min	40m
MODERATE		Good

▶ LEG 12.2.R

To junction with off-road		
5km	15min	40m

▶ LEG 12.3.OR

To junction with N-630		
10km	1hr 40min	100m
CHALLENGING		Good

▶ LEG 12.3.R

To junction with off-road		
9km	40min	100m

▶ LEG 12.4.R

To junction with off-road		
10km	35min	110m

▶ LEG 12.5.OR

To Pola de Lena		
41km	3hr 20min	-900m
CHALLENGING		Excellent

▶ LEG 12.5.R

To Pola de Lena		
33km	1hr 45min	-900m

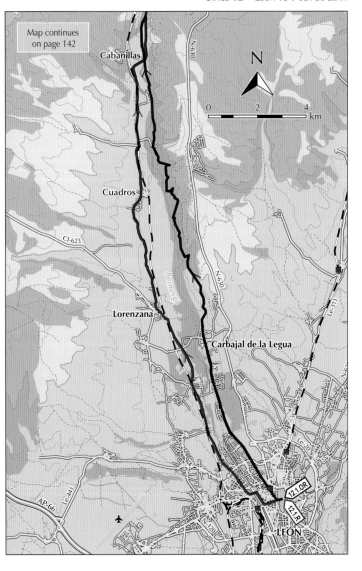

Map continues on page 142

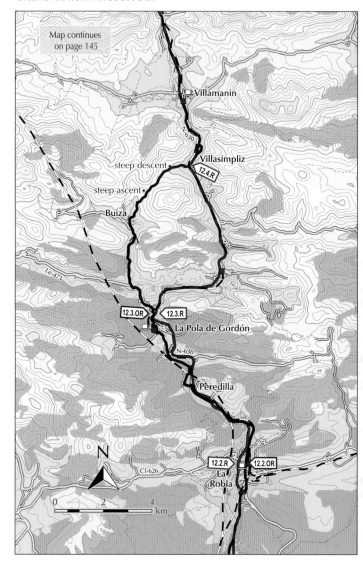

Map continues
on page 145

Villamanín

N-630

steep descent

Villasimpliz

12.4.R

steep ascent

Buiza

Le-473

12.3.OR

12.3.R

La Pola de Gordón

N-630

Peredilla

N

Cl-626

0   2   4
km

12.2.R

12.2.OR

La
Robla

Stage 12: Road route

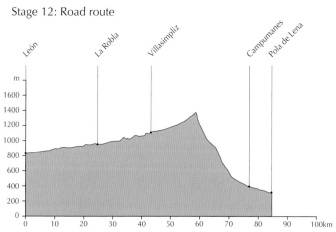

ROAD ROUTE

Leg 12.1.R to La Robla

From the cathedral go west along the Calle Ancha, take the third exit at a large roundabout and continue over a second roundabout to the square in front of the parador. Cross the bridge, continue to the roundabout and take the first exit. Continue north along a fairly busy road (the CL-623) parallel with the river. At **Lorenzana**, reached after 10km, join a smaller country road and follow it north along the valley through the village of **Cuadros** before crossing the river at **Cabanillas** and joining the N-630 just south of **La Robla**.

Leg 12.2.R to junction with off-road

Continue along the **N-630**, which runs just west of La Robla, to the junction north of **La Pola de Gordón**.

Leg 12.3.R to Villasimpliz

Take the N-630 and continue up a tight valley, with tunnels, through a series of small mining villages to **Villasimpliz**.

Leg 12.4.R to junction with off-road

Go north on the N-630 past **Villamanin** (good roadside restaurant for refreshments) and continue for 6km to the junction with the off-road route.

Leg 12.5.R to Pola de Lena

Continue on the N-630 up to the **pass** 'Llana de Puerto', which, if you're lucky with the weather, is a brilliant place to take photographs. There is a restaurant on the roadside if you are hungry. The switchbacking road descending rapidly down from the pass is excellent, but watch out for ascending slow-moving lorries which swing out wide on the U bends. After 18km, and a descent of 1000m **Campumanes** is reached. At Campumanes the route leaves the N-630 (which merges with the motorway) and follows a side road to **Pola de Lena**. Just beyond the village is a lovely hotel, the Hotel Rural El Reundu, much favoured with the locals and excellent for lunch.

OFF-ROAD (CAMINO) ROUTE

Leg 12.1.OR to La Robla

The road and off-road routes from León to La Robla are completely different. The off-road route follows a ridge on the eastern side of a valley with occasional tough stretches of cycling. There are pilgrim waymarks all the way to La Robla.

From the cathedral, head west along the Calle Ancha to a large roundabout and take the exit into the Calle de Padra Isla. Stay on this road for 7km as it heads north out of town (crossing a roundabout after 2km) to **Carbajal de la Legua** where the road turns into an agricultural track. Continue north along an increasingly undulating track (occasionally single track) where some pushing may be needed. From the small village of **Cabanillas**, reached after 8km, follow a riverside trail for 4km to a road which takes you to **La Robla**. A footbridge has to be negotiated on the final approach to the town centre.

Leg 12.2.OR to junction with N-630

From the centre of La Robla go north for 4km along a quiet road to **Peredilla**, turn left north of the village and pass underneath the N-630. Follow a track running alongside the railway for 1km then turn left and cross the railway and a bridge over a river. Turn right onto a track and follow this to **La Pola de Gordón** (refreshments available). Pass through the village to meet up with the N-630 on its northern side.

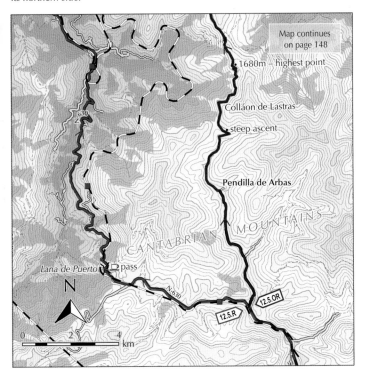

Descending into the Asturias

Looking back along the Via Romana de la Carisa (off-road route)

Leg 12.3.OR to junction with N-630

Bear left at the junction with the N-630 onto a road going northwest for 2km, then turn right onto a smaller country road and follow it for 3km to the village of **Buiza**.

Stage 12: Off-road route

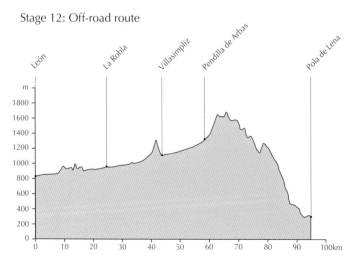

Ignoring the Camino markers, bear right at the church and take an agricultural track underneath a large power line, east up a valley. Continue on an increasingly steep track up to the pass and then descend a steep, occasionally concreted track to **Villasimpliz** and the junction with the N-630.

Leg 12.4.R to junction with off-road

Join the road and follow Leg 12.4.R as described in the road route.

Leg 12.5.OR to Pola de Lena

This final stretch of off-road is demanding, but spectacular.

Turn right off the N-630 and follow a quiet country road up a valley to the tiny settlement of **Pendilla de Arbas**, where the Roman road, the Via Romana de la Carisa, starts. Turning left at the settlement, follow an agricultural track up a

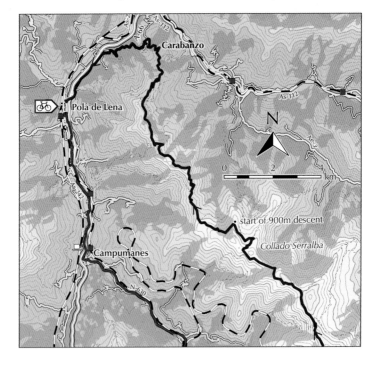

The tiny church of Santa Cristina de Lena

valley with the route getting particularly steep as it zig-zags its way up to the pass, the **Colláon de Lastras** (1650m). Swinging round a saddle, the route continues to climb, reaching its **highest point (1680m)** after another 3km. At 4km from the pass the route reaches a junction with another route. Turn sharp left, heading backwards and downhill before turning right again and continuing north along the western side of the ridge. After 2km bear left at another junction and continue on a descending route for another 10km to a pass, the Collado Serralba. Here the route switches to the eastern side of the ridge and climbs again, before starting a 900m descent. The surface is mixed, mainly gravel with the occasional stretches of concrete, but the route is always wide enough to accommodate a vehicle making navigation around any damaged parts easy. A proper metalled road is reached at **Carabanzo** from where it turns west and heads down to **Pola de Lena**.

POLA DE LENA

There is not a lot to see in Pola de Lena itself, but it's a good place to rest up. The most local important building, the tiny pre-Romanesque Santa Cristina de Lena, is located a few miles to the south and perhaps best visited the next day. The Hotel Ruta de la Plata is good value and for food, try the very friendly Restaurante Filanguiru. For pilgrimage-style accommodation go to the Albergue de Peregrinos (tel +34 985 49 22 47).

STAGE 13
Pola de Lena to Oviedo

Start	Pola de Lena
Distance	Road 36km, off-road 37km
Ascent	Road 1140m, off-road 1040m
Descent	Road 1220, off-road 1120m
Time	Road 2hr 30min, off-road 3hr 30min

Strong cyclists will be able to combine Stages 13 and 14 and make it all the way to Gijón but that would mean missing out on Oviedo, a beautiful and historic city.

The road and off-road routes to Oviedo are entirely separate, with each navigating a busy transport corridor in different ways. The road route makes a better job of it and after a tough climb out of the valley follows a pleasant and empty road along another valley before rejoining the N-630 for the final run to Oviedo. The off-road route, which for most part follows metalled roads, avoids the big climb but is not as good.

Both routes, although relatively short, involve significant ascent and descent. The road route is slightly harder but after a tough 500m climb out the valley the rest will feel easy. The off-road route has almost the same amount of total ascent and descent but none of the climbs exceed 200m.

ROAD ROUTE (RECOMMENDED)

From the main square in the centre of Pola de Lena follow the one-way system north and continue on the same road out of town. After 1km, turn left under a railway line, continue to the village of **Muñón Fondiru** and then follow a steeply climbing road up to the pass. From the pass take a lovely descending road to the village of **L'Ará**, a good place to stop for refreshments. From L'Ará take the main road (AS-231) northeast out of town which sticks close to the river and runs through a tight and pretty gorge. Turn left onto the **N-630** and continue north for 5km, crossing two rivers. At the second roundabout after the second river crossing leave the N-630 (for the last time), cross the motorway and three roundabouts. At a fourth roundabout take the fourth exit and follow the Carretera de la Bolgachina all the way into **Oviedo** (watch for a left turn at **El Caserón**).

Stage 13: Road route

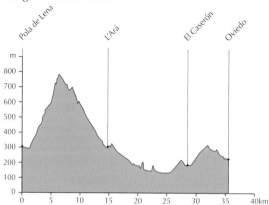

San Julián de los Prados

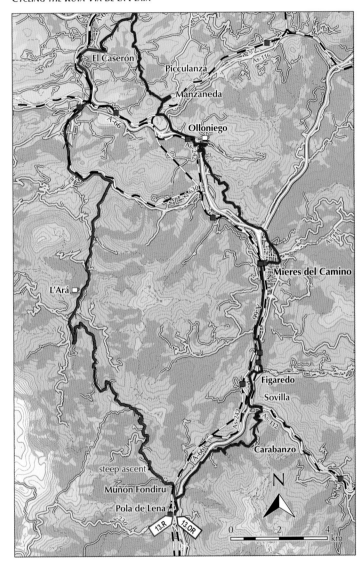

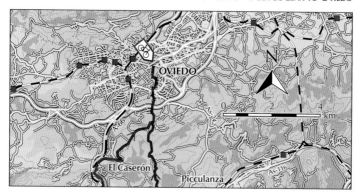

OFF-ROAD (CAMINO) ROUTE

From the main square in Pola de Lena follow the one-way system north. Take a right-hand turn, cross the roundabout, go over the river and motorway and follow the road uphill to **Carabanzo** (retracing yesterday's final leg) and down to Sovilla. Turn right at the bottom of the hill and left shortly after. Head down to a roundabout and join a cycle path on its opposite side. Follow the path west, under the motorway and north along the side of a river into **Figaredo** and join the road heading north. Follow the road for 1.5km, turn left onto a smaller road and cross a bridge over the river.

Continue north along the river (sometimes on the road, sometimes on the cycle path) for 3km and cross the river into the busy town of **Mieres del Camino**. Go north through the town and follow the AS-242 for 6km to Olloniego climbing

Stage 13: Off-road route

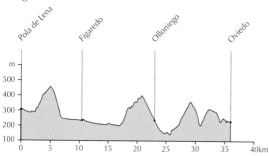

153

out of one valley into another. Go through **Olloneigo**, bear left on the outskirts, pass underneath the motorway and climb up to the hillside village of **Manzaneda**. Turn right on the outskirts of the village then right again and continue climbing up to another even smaller village (Picullanza) which sits on a pass.

Continue through the village (ignoring a left turn) and following a narrow descending road that turns into what is at times at challenging track. At the end of the descent the route joins a metalled road which can be followed all the way into **Oviedo**.

OVIEDO

With a different climate and a distinct architectural legacy, Oviedo (pop 220,000) feels different from other RVP towns and cities. Its medieval core, much of which is pedestrianised, makes it a lovely place to visit.

The city was founded in the late 8th century and was chosen by King Alfonso I as the capital of the Kingdom of the Asturias, the only part Iberian peninsula not dominated at the time by Muslims. The first churches were built employing a style related to provincial Roman and known as pre-Romanesque. Oviedo was on the newly opened Camino route, and money from pilgrims flowed into city for two centuries. Once León became the capital of Asturias (with the death of Alfonso III, 'the Great'), Oviedo lost some of its political significance but it continued to develop as a medieval city.

Oviedo's big draw is its pre-Romanesque buildings which have been awarded UNESCO World Heritage Site status. They also attracted the interest of Woody Allen in his film *Vicky Cristina Barcelona* and a grateful city erected a statue in his honour. These buildings however are scattered around the city. The two most accessible examples are the Cámara Santa de Oviedo, located inside the cathedral and the San Julián de los Prados located in a small park about 15 mins walk from the cathedral. San Julián de los Prados is more interesting, but only open at certain times.

There isn't a parador in Oviedo but there are plenty of alternatives and the Hotel de la Reconquista is a good substitute. I stayed at Ayre Hotel Ramiro I which was comfortable and good value. For pilgrimage-style accommodation consider the Albergue de Peregrinos de Oviedo (tel +34 985 22 85 25) or the Albergue Turistico La Peregrina (tel +34 687 13 39 32).

Oviedo is the place on the RVP to drink cider if for no other reason than to witness it being served with style, panache and remarkable accuracy. A good place to try it, and sample excellent local food presented in modern way is at La Finca, a local 'agrobar'.

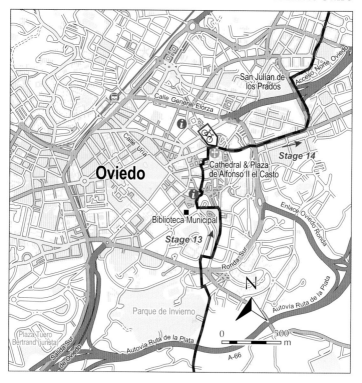

STAGE 14
Oviedo to Gijón

Start	Oviedo
Distance	Road 44km, off-road 36km
Ascent	Road 520m, off-road 430m
Descent	Road 750m, off-road 660m
Time	Road 3hr 15min, off-road 3hr 40min

The last stage is easy one and travels through a landscape where small-scale livestock farming sits cheek by jowl with heavy industry. Both road and off-road routes can be cycled with a road bike, with the off-road more direct and preferable if you don't want to see the steel mills near Gijón and the open-air archaeological museum at the Campo de Torres. Not only is the off-road route shorter, it has just under half the ascent of the road route.

Apart from the departure from Oviedo the two routes are independent of each other, so as with Stage 13 there are no leg descriptions. Navigation out of Oviedo and through a dense network of country lanes to Gijón is both complicated and hard to describe; the routes are, however, easy to follow with a GPS strapped to your handlebars.

ROAD ROUTE

Join the one-way system north of the cathedral (the Calle Azcárraga) and go east across a busy junction and along the N-634. Bear left at the first junction, left again at the roundabout and take the first exit at the next roundabout. Navigating eight roundabouts, cross first three, take the third exit at the fourth, cross the fifth, take the second exit at the sixth and seventh and the first exit at the eighth.

Continue for 3.5km, turn left (in **Llugones**) and continue for 3km to join the **AS-17**. Follow it northwest, turning right at the first junction and continue for 2km to **Lugo de Llanera**. Take the first left on the edge of the village and turn left again in front of the town hall. Climbing now go north then east for 3km, take a sharp left, and then descend to a junction with a main road and turn right.

Follow the **AS-325** for 5km and take a sharp left-hand turn up to an old railway. Turn right and use the **railway bridge** to cross the motorway underneath. Turn

Stage 14: Road route

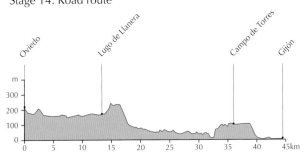

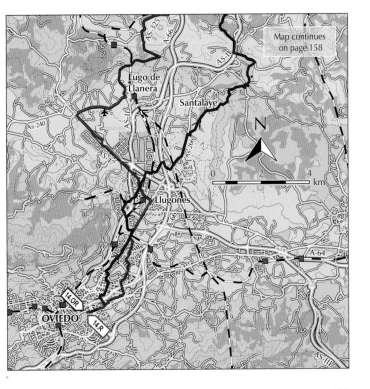

Map continues
on page 158

157

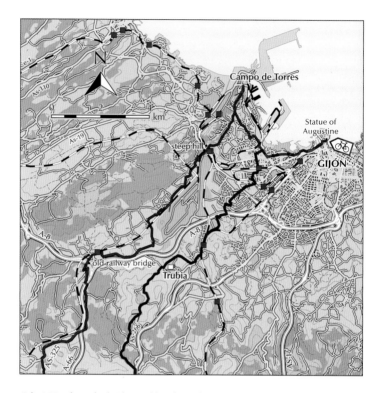

right 800m from the bridge and head east for 2km. Cross the first roundabout and turn left at the second, cross the third, turn right at the forth and right again at the fifth. Follow a small road northwest for 4km skirting round a huge steel works and after crossing underneath a railway line, turn left onto a busy road and then immediately right. Follow another small road up a savagely **steep hill** for 1km then turn left and continue for 3km to **Campo de Torres**.

To get to Gijón, return along the same road from Campo de Torres and take an oblique right turn after 1km. Descend steeply along a narrow road for 1km and left turn as the road levels out, then take the next right onto a larger road down to a roundabout. Cross the roundabout and follow the N-641 for 600m. Turn left at a major junction and take the coastal road all the way to the Plaza Mayor in **Gijón**.

OFF-ROAD ROUTE (RECOMMENDED)

The off-road route leaves Oviedo on the same route as the road route.

Join the one-way system north of the cathedral (the Calle Azcárraga) and go head east across a busy junction on the N-634. Bear left at the first junction, left again at the roundabout and take the first exit at the next roundabout. Navigating eight roundabouts, cross first three, take the third exit at the fourth, cross the fifth, take the second exit at the sixth and seventh and the first exit at the eighth.

Continue for 2km and after passing underneath a railway take the first left, follow a small road northeast alongside a canal for 1km before turning right over a canal bridge. Continue northeast, turn left at the next junction, cross a railway bridge and continue east for another kilometre before turning left at a junction. Continue on this road for 800m, turn right then left, pass underneath the motorway and turn right and, after passing underneath a railway, turn left. Continue northeast, pass underneath the motorway, turn right and at the next junction (a complex set of roundabouts) turn left onto **AS-266**.

Follow this for just under 2km before turning right onto a small country road. After 50m or so take a sharp left, continue down to **Santalaye** (a modern suburb), turn right, and continue for 800m before turning right again. Ignoring two right-hand turns continue to a junction for 800m and turn right. Continue for another 800m, turn left and immediately right again onto an easy semi-metalled agricultural track.

The agricultural track lasts for 1.5km and can be avoided by staying on the road and joining the AS-266 until it passes underneath the motorway to the foot-bridge described below.

After joining the agricultural track take a sharp left after 50m and head north taking the second left onto a road. Continue west and as the road swings north leave it and take a footbridge over the motorway to turn right onto the AS-266.

Stage 14: Off-road route

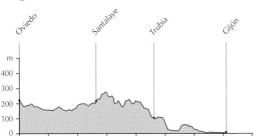

Augustine's statue in Gijón marks the end of the route

After 500m take a left turn onto a smaller road and follow it for 5km, ignoring turns to the left and right, until you reach a left turn-off to **Trubia** where refreshments can be found.

Leaving Trubia, take a right turn after 800m and then turn left to rejoin the road used before the Trubia excursion. Continue north and pass underneath a motorway before turning right towards Gijón. There are many ways into Gijón but the official route turns left just after crossing a railway, follows a cycle route underneath a railway line, and then turns right into the Calle Brasil, turns right and through a small park, onto the Calle Mariano Pola which can then be followed along the sea front to the marina and the Plaza Mayor in **Gijón**.

The **statue to Augustine** – which marks the end of the RVP – is on the eastern side of the Plaza Mayor.

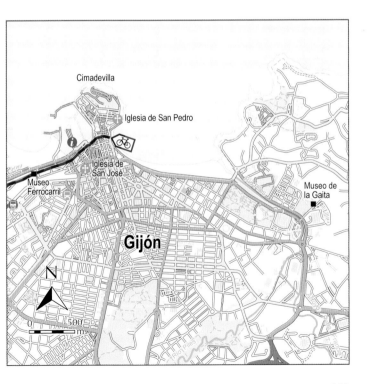

GIJÓN

Plaza del Ayuntamiento, Gijón

Gijón can trace its history back to pre-Roman times but its current prominence, the largest city in the Asturias, dates to the late 19C and the rapid industrialisation of northern Spain. It's success enabled the construction of a large port, originally built to import coal to power the iron and steel works firstly in Avilés and then in Gijón itself. As well as iron and steel, the city became Spain's most important ship building centre. At the same time, Gijón established itself as a seaside destination for daytrippers from Oviedo. The reliance on heavy industry proved a weakness and the city suffered an employment crisis in the 1980s and establishing a more diversified economy has been a long term project.

The historic centre of the city is small. It's built behind a peninsular seperating a huge sweeping beach to the east and the port to the west. Walking round the penisular, past the Roman Baths, up to artwork, the 'Eulogy to the Horizon' by Eduardo Chillida and down to original fishing port is a good way to spend time before having a final dinner near the Plaza Mayor.

For accommodation consider the Parador de Gijón located in a park to the east of the city centre or the Hotel Marqués located near the marina. For traditional Asturian food served in a modern way, go to Restaurante La Cuadra de Antón located near the Plaza Mayor. For pilgrimage-style accommodation try the Albergue Merendero El Peregrin (tel +34 652 76 76 01).

CAMINO SANABRÉS

Spanish guacho on the Camino Sanabrés (Stage 2)

STAGE 1S
Zamora to Tábara

Start	Zamora
Distance	Road 61km, off-road 68km, hybrid 62km
Ascent	Road 470m, off-road 520m
Descent	Road 380m, off road 430m
Time	Road 4hr 20min, off-road 5hr 20min, hybrid 4hr 45min
Hybrid route	Leg 10.1.OR → Leg 10.2.R → Leg 1.1.R → Leg 1.2.R → Leg 1.3.R

The Camino Sanabrés splits from the RVP at Granja de Moreruela, about 40km into Stage 10. Tábara is another 25km further on. The timings and distances above assume the start point was Zamora.

The first part of the Camino Sanabrés is easy, a gentle journey with one short hill climb, through a wide-open arable landscape. There isn't much to do in Tábara so consider visiting the ruins of the Cisterian Moreruela Abbey, en route to the west of Granja de Moreruela – it's a great place for a picnic.

The route descriptions to Granja de Moreruela are provided in the description of the Ruta Vía de la Plata.

ROAD ROUTE

Leg 10.1.R to Montamarta
This is the same as the Ruta Vía de la Plata. Take the northeast exit from the Plaza Mayor and follow the one-way system down to a roundabout, join the **N-630** and follow it to **Montamarta**.

Leg 10.2.R to Granja de Moreruela
This is the same as the Ruta Vía de la Plata. Continue north on the N-630, crossing the motorway twice, to **Granja de Moreruela**, which has bars for refreshments. The Camino Sanabrés leaves the RVP here.

Stage 1S (Sanabrés): Zamora to Tábara

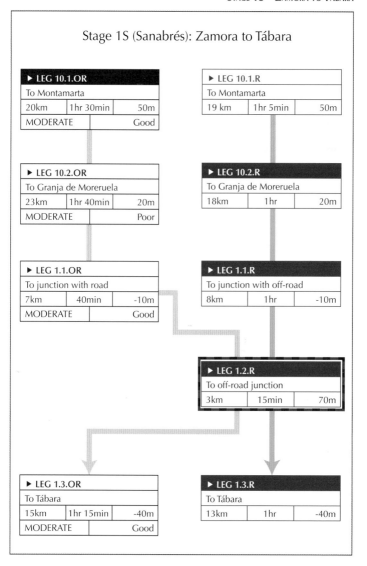

▶ LEG 10.1.OR
To Montamarta
| 20km | 1hr 30min | 50m |
| MODERATE | | Good |

▶ LEG 10.1.R
To Montamarta
| 19 km | 1hr 5min | 50m |

▶ LEG 10.2.OR
To Granja de Moreruela
| 23km | 1hr 40min | 20m |
| MODERATE | | Poor |

▶ LEG 10.2.R
To Granja de Moreruela
| 18km | 1hr | 20m |

▶ LEG 1.1.OR
To junction with road
| 7km | 40min | -10m |
| MODERATE | | Good |

▶ LEG 1.1.R
To junction with off-road
| 8km | 1hr | -10m |

▶ LEG 1.2.R
To off-road junction
| 3km | 15min | 70m |

▶ LEG 1.3.OR
To Tábara
| 15km | 1hr 15min | -40m |
| MODERATE | | Good |

▶ LEG 1.3.R
To Tábara
| 13km | 1hr | -40m |

165

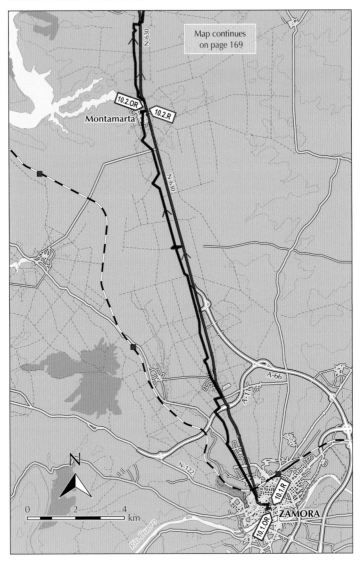

Map continues on page 169

N-630

10.2.OR

10.2.R

Montamarta

N-630

A-66

A-11

N-122

10.1.R

10.1.OR

ZAMORA

Río Duero

N

0   2   4 km

Stage 1S: Road route

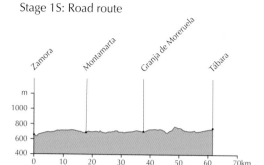

Leg 1.1.R to junction with off-road

From **Granja de Moreruela**, continue north along the **N-630** for 2km and, after an emotional farewell, turn left and go downhill to the junction with the off-road route.

Leg 1.2.R to off-road junction

The road and off-road routes combine for 3km as the Camino, heading along the western shore of the Río Esla, is inaccessible for bikes.

Continue down the hill, across a bridge over the Río Esla and start a 70m climb for 3km to a left-hand junction with a smaller country road. The road route stays on the main road.

Leg 1.3.R to Tábara

Stay on the main road and continue southwest and down and through **Faramontanos de Tábara** to the **N631**, turn right and head up to **Tábara**.

OFF-ROAD (CAMINO) ROUTE

Leg 10.1.OR to Montamarta

This is the same as the Ruta Vía de la Plata. Take the northeast exit from the Plaza Mayor and follow the one-way system down to a roundabout. Join the N-122, go up a hill for 200m and take an oblique left turn into the Calle de la Hiniesta. Continue for 3km, turn right onto an agricultural road and after passing under a motorway take a sharp right. Turn left after 100m, then right, then left again reaching a roundabout and the N-630. Follow an agricultural road that tracks the N-630 all the way to **Montamarta**.

Leg 10.2.OR to Granja de Moreruela

This is the same as the Ruta Vía de la Plata. Leg 10.2 is not difficult, but it is ugly and, with long stretches of gravel track running immediately next to either the N-630 or the new motorway, the road route is recommended instead.

For off-road, cross the bridge from Montamarta, turn left onto a dirt track and follow it climbing north away from the reservoir. Continue for 4km before turning abruptly east (some re-routing here) and cross the motorway via a bridge. Continue north on a gravel track around a complex intersection before crossing the motorway again. After passing the ruins of a castle (the Pilares de Castro) continue north to the village of **Riego del Camino** and on to **Granja de Moreruela**. For cyclists on the Camino Sanabrés, this is where the route leaves the RVP – see Leg 1.1.OR of the Camino Sanabrés to continue.

Leg 1.1.OR to junction with road

Leave **Granja de Moreruela** on an agricultural track heading west, pass under the motorway and turn right 200m later. To visit the monastery of **Moreruela Abbey**, don't turn right but continue heading west for nearly 1km, then take a left turn down to a road and then right. If not visiting Moreruela Abbey, head northwest for 1.5km, turn right, climb over a hill and go down to the road.

Leg 1.2.R to off-road junction

Join the road and follow Leg 1.2.R as described in the road route.

Leg 1.3.OR to Tábara

Turn left and follow a quiet road for 2km before turning right onto an agricultural track. Continue for 500m and turn left (easily missed), going southwest for 2km. Ignore the first right-hand turn, take the second and follow a dead straight

Stage 1S: Off-road route

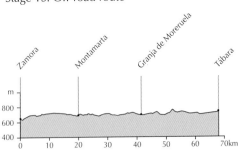

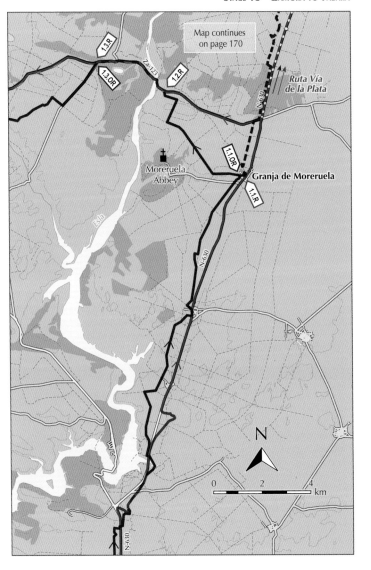

Map continues
on page 170

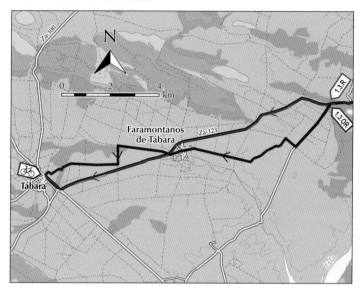

agricultural track into the village of **Faramontanos de Tábara**. Go west through the village and cross the main road on its western side to join another agricultural track. Continue west for 2km then turn left, then right 600m later. Continue west to **Tábara**, crossing the new TGV line on the way.

TÁBARA

Tábara is a small town with a lot of bars, a large Romanesque church and a hotel. The Hotel El Roble is not on Booking.com but responds to email – elrobletabara@gmail.com. It provides simple accommodation and also has a restaurant. Pilgrimage-style accommodation is also available at the municipal *albergue* (tel +34 637 926 068).

STAGE 2S

Tábara to Puebla de Sanabria

Start	Tábara
Distance	Road 86km, off-road 97km, hybrid 95km
Ascent	Road 670m, off-road 930m
Descent	Road 490m, off-road 750m
Time	Road 4hr 55min, off-road 7hr 45min, hybrid 7hr 10min
Hybrid route	Leg 2.1.OR → Leg 2.2.OR →Leg 2.3.OR →Leg 2.4.OR →Leg 2.5.R →Leg 2.6.R →Leg 2.7.R →

Stage 2, despite its length and accumulated ascent, is not challenging and, providing off-roaders adopt the hybrid route, there are no significant climbs or descents.

After navigating quiet country roads and reaching the River Tera, the road route joins a quiet and gently ascending N-525. There are lots of roadside places to stop for refreshments, reflecting a time when the route was much busier.

The first four legs of the off-road provide good cycling, with the second leg, which follows the River Tera, particularly good. The landscape is generally varied, switching between arable, woodland and scrub. Legs 5, 6 and 7 are short and all run very close to the N-525. The fifth leg is particularly unpleasant and after a long day, all of them could be avoided.

Please note that at the time of researching this book, the TGV remained under construction. All the crossings were in place, but it is possible that small changes might be made once the railway becomes operational.

There are plenty of places on the route to stop for refreshments, but the Me Gusta Comer at Rionegro del Puente is particularly nice.

Stage 2S (Sanabrés): Tábara to Puebla de Sanabria

▶ LEG 2.1.OR		
To Santa Marta de Tera		
24km	1hr 50min	-10m
MODERATE		Good

▶ LEG 2.1.R		
To Santa Marta de Tera		
27km	1hr 40min	-10m

▶ LEG 2.2.OR		
To Rionegro del Puente		
29km	2hr 10min	60m
DIFFICULT		Excellent

▶ LEG 2.2.R		
To Rionegro del Puente		
23km	1hr 15min	60m

▶ LEG 2.3.OR		
To Mombuey		
11km	55min	90m
MODERATE		Good

▶ LEG 2.3.R		
To Mombuey		
10km	35min	90m

▶ LEG 2.4.OR		
To Asturianos		
18km	1hr 30min	80m
DIFFICULT		Good

▶ LEG 2.4.R		
To Asturianos		
13km	40min	80m

▶ LEG 2.5.OR		
To Palacios de Sanabria		
3km	20min	10m
CHALLENGING		Poor

▶ LEG 2.5.R		
To Palacios de Sanabria		
3km	10min	10m

▶ LEG 2.6.OR		
To Otero de Sanabria		
5km	25min	-10m
DIFFICULT		Poor

▶ LEG 2.6.R		
To Otero de Sanabria		
4km	15min	-10m

▶ LEG 2.7.OR		
To Puebla de Sanabria		
7km	35min	-50m
DIFFICULT		Poor

▶ LEG 2.7.R		
To Puebla de Sanabria		
6km	20min	-50m

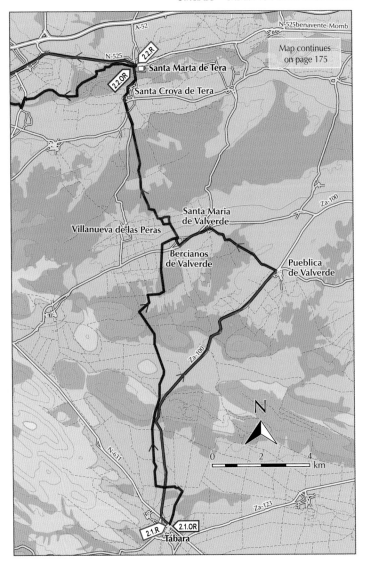

Map continues
on page 175

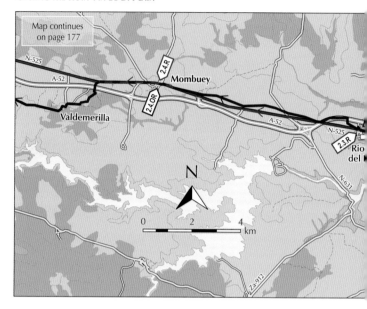

ROAD ROUTE

Leg 2.1.R to Santa Marta de Tera
Go northwest from the church along the main road to the first junction. Turn right and join the **ZA-100**, heading northwest. After 13km turn left at a junction in the village of **Pueblica de Valverde** and continue for 3km to **Santa Marìa de Valverde**. Turn left into the centre of the village and continue. On reaching **Bercianos de Valverde**, turn left and go north to **Santa Croya de Tera** and on, over the river, to **Santa Marta de Tera**.

Leg 2.2.R to Rionegro del Puente
Continue west on the **N-525**. The route passes through a series of villages, all of which have bars and cafés, before arriving in **Rionegro del Puente**.

Leg 2.3.R to Mombuey
Continue west on the N-525 to **Mombuey**, crossing the motorway en route.

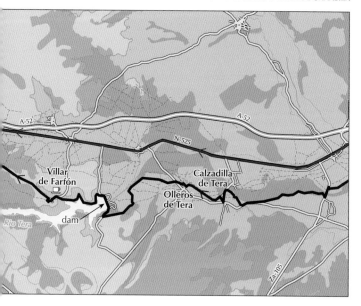

Leg 2.4.R to Asturianos
Continue on the N-525 to **Asturianos**.

Leg 2.5.R to Palacios de Sanabria
Continue on the N-525 to **Palacios de Sanabria**.

Stage 2S: Road route

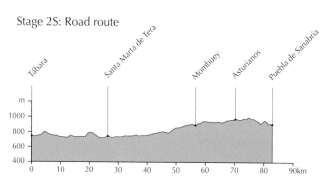

175

The alternative to the Camino Sanabrés – the empty N-525

Leg 2.6.R to Otero de Sanabria
Continue on the N-525 to **Otero de Sanabria**.

Leg 2.7.R to Puebla de Sanabria
Follow the N-525 to a roundabout, take the third exit and head down to **Puebla de Sanabria**.

OFF-ROAD (CAMINO) ROUTE

Leg 2.1.OR to Santa Marta de Tera
Cross the road near the church and follow the track north to the new railway. Turn left, cross the road and then turn right onto an agricultural track. Continue north for 7km to a junction. Turn right, then left at the next junction 600m later, then right at the next junction 300m later, and finally left 600m later. Continue north for 2km, cross a road and turn right into the village of **Bercianos de Valverde**. Turn left onto a road and follow it north to **Santa Croya de Tera** and on, over the river, to **Santa Marta de Tera**.

Leg 2.2.OR to Rionegro del Puente
Take a sharp left immediately before entering the main square in Santa Marta de Tera and go west on

Stage 2S: Off-road route

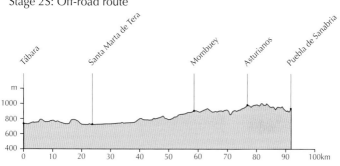

a track. Turn left after 500m and go down to the river. Take the north bank of the river to a road, cross the river via a bridge, then take the first turn right and on a track for 3km to a road. Follow this road for 300m, then turn right and continue on to a track alongside a canal for 1km. Turn left into **Calzadilla de Tera**. The route goes up into the village before returning to the canal, a bridge and a track on its north side.

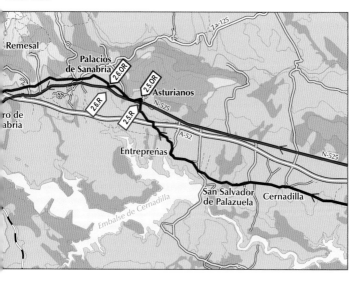

Follow the canal-side track for 1.5km and cross a bridge into **Olleros de Tera**. Go through the village and over a crossroads to a track and follow it for 3km. Take a right turn at a junction and continue west for 2km to a road. Turn right and go down to a **dam** and a reservoir. Take the first left and follow a reservoir side path to **Villar de Farfón**. Take a sharp right on the far side of the village and follow signs to an auberge (refreshments available). From the auberge, follow a track – occasionally single track – across moorland to join the **N-525** heading into **Rionegro del Puente**.

Leg 2.3.OR to Mombuey
Join an agricultural track west out of the village over and alongside the motorway, and then across open grazing land to the village of **Mombuey**. If lucky you'll see riders watching over a herd of cattle gaucho-style.

Leg 2.4.OR to Asturianos
Follow the N-525 for about 600m and turn left onto a track. After 300m cross a junction with a road, then continue on the track as it runs parallel with the N-525. After about 2km turn south and cross the motorway, then the new TGV railway, before reaching **Valdemerilla**. Continue west on a small road/track connecting the villages of **Cernadilla** and **San Salvador de Palazuela** and stay on a narrow track to a road going through **Entrepreñas**. Turn left on the road just north of the village and follow a track to **Asturianos**, crossing the railway and motorway in the process.

Leg 2.5.OR to Palacios de Sanabria
This short 3km stretch running north of the N-525 is both difficult and unpleasant. To find it, continue along the N-525 for 200m and then turn right along a road and left onto a track about 100m later. Follow an overgrown and possibly wet track almost back to the N-525, turn right and continue on the track to **Palacios de Sanabria**.

Leg 2.6.OR to Otero de Sanabria
Join a track immediately to the west of the church. Follow it to and through the village of Remesal and down towards the motorway. Take the track west alongside the motorway, take the bridge over it and go down to **Otero de Sanabria**.

Leg 2.7.OR to Puebla de Sanabria
Turn right onto a road on the west side of Otero de Sanabria and head north underneath the motorway. Continue to Triufe, then take a left turn going back to the motorway. Cross a bridge and go down to the N-525, follow it to a roundabout, take the third exit and head down to **Puebla de Sanabria**.

Anyone lost a tractor?

PUEBLA DE SANABRIA

Maybe it's the slate roofs, the granite stone used in buildings, or the fact that it was raining and unseasonably cold during a visit to research this book, but Puebla de Sanabria feels like a mountain town. It has a lovely hilltop location, dominated by a castle, and feels austere.

The town was founded in the 6th century. The castle was built in the 15th century by the Count of Benavente, although the church is older. The cobbled streets, half-timbered houses, the castle and a walk along city walls make for a pleasant if short pre-dinner sortie.

The parador is inconvenient if you want to explore the town. There are plenty of accommodation options on Booking.com, but the Posada de las Misas is excellent and apparently has the town's best restaurant. For pilgrimage-style accommodation, consider the private Casa Luz (www.albergue-casaluz.es). For cosy, good value food and cider try the Sidreria La Guaja.

STAGE 3S
Puebla de Sanabria to A Gudiña

Start	Puebla de Sanabria
Distance	Road 59km, off-road 53km, hybrid 59km
Ascent	Road 1230m, off-road 1330m
Descent	Road 1170m, off-road 1270m
Time	Road 3hr 55min, off-road 4hr 55min, hybrid 4hr
Hybrid route	Leg 3.1.OR → Leg 3.2.R → Leg 3.3.R → Leg 3.4.R → Leg 3.5.R

On Stage 3 the Camino Sanabrés heads decisively up into the mountains. The valley narrows and passes get steeper. In remote countryside the villages are smaller and agriculture marginal, with wooded hillsides the dominant feature. However, the transport corridor is busy, even congested. As well as the ancient Camino, it now features a brand-new motorway, a new TGV, and the N-525, all of which come together at or under a series of passes.

The recommended hybrid route is just under 60km and will take around four hours to complete. It only includes one off-road leg (much of which is on a sealed surface) and involves a lot a road cycling. The other two off-road legs, both of which follow the Camino, are difficult. The first includes a steep ascent to the pass, much of which is in undergrowth and along a narrow track. It is both challenging and unpleasant. The second follows a pretty route, but it is challenging, with a lot of difficult single track. Avoiding these two off-road sections shortens the day significantly and turns a difficult day into an easy one, albeit with some climbing.

There is not much (anything) to do at A Gudiña so there is no need to rush. Lubián is about halfway and the Bar Javi is a nice place for lunch.

ROAD ROUTE

Leg 3.1.R to Requejo
From the junction at the southern end of the old town in Puebla de Sanabria turn left, head back towards the bridge and continue underneath the walls around the town, crossing a bridge on its western side. Follow the road to join the **N-525** into **Requejo**.

Stage 3S (Sanabrés): Puebla de Sanabria to A Gudiña

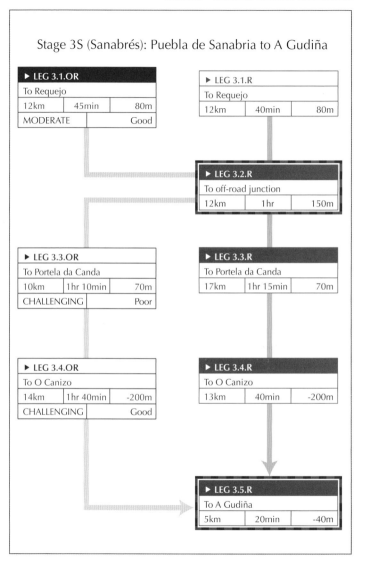

▶ LEG 3.1.OR

To Requejo

12km	45min	80m
MODERATE		Good

▶ LEG 3.1.R

To Requejo

12km	40min	80m

▶ LEG 3.2.R

To off-road junction

12km	1hr	150m

▶ LEG 3.3.OR

To Portela da Canda

10km	1hr 10min	70m
CHALLENGING		Poor

▶ LEG 3.3.R

To Portela da Canda

17km	1hr 15min	70m

▶ LEG 3.4.OR

To O Canizo

14km	1hr 40min	-200m
CHALLENGING		Good

▶ LEG 3.4.R

To O Canizo

13km	40min	-200m

▶ LEG 3.5.R

To A Gudiña

5km	20min	-40m

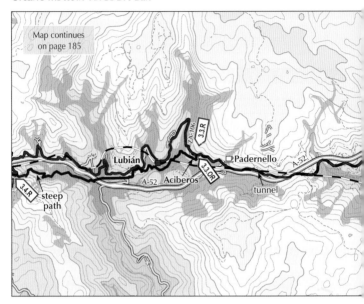

Leg 3.2.R to off-road junction

At Requejo the road and off-road routes combine on the N-525 and start a steady 300m climb to the pass. At the top of the pass the route passes through a **tunnel** before descending to **Padernello** where refreshments are available. About 2km

Stage 3S: Road route

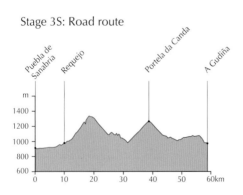

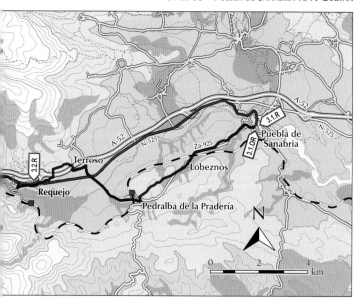

after Padernello, the N-525 merges with the motorway, so take a right turn, and join the **ZA-106**. The off-road turn-off is 2km further on.

Leg 3.3.R to Portela da Canda

Take the ZA-106 as it contours its way to **Lubián**. Continue through the village. After 3km the road reaches a junction with the N-525 which is no longer merged with the motorway and can be rejoined. The ZA-106 provides a more scenic, but less direct route up to the pass at **Portela da Canda**.

Leg 3.4.R to O Canizo

Go down the hill from the pass and join the N-525 after 2km. Continue along the N-525, which has a number of roadside restaurants, to the junction with the off-road at **O Canizo**.

Leg 3.5.R to A Gudiña

For the last 5km the road and off-road routes combine, so follow the N-525 to **A Gudiña**.

OFF-ROAD (CAMINO) ROUTE

Leg 3.1.OR to Requejo
At the time of writing the Camino was closed due to the construction of the TGV and the off-road route follows an alternative course to Requejo along small country roads.

Go from the southern end of the old town in Puebla de Sanabria (ie don't head down towards the bridge) go south to a roundabout and take the first exit. Continue west through the village of **Lobeznos**, turn right after 500m onto a track to **Pedralba de la Pradería**. Pass through the village, continue northwest and, 1km after passing under the N-525 turn left into **Terroso**. Turn right in the centre of the village and take a track over a bridge crossing the motorway. After 200m, turn left at a junction and follow a track back over the motorway and into the village of **Requejo**.

Leg 3.2.R to off-road junction
Join the road and follow Leg 3.2.R as described in the road route.

Leg 3.3.OR to Portela da Canda
The second half of Leg 3.3.OR is really difficult.

Turn left off the ZA-106 and descend to **Aciberos**. Head through the village and join a dirt track on its western side. Follow the track down the hillside and over a railway, then continue west through small fields into **Lubián**. Take the road

Stage 3S: Off-road route

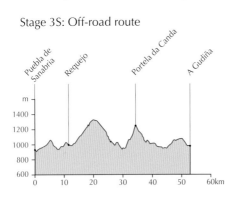

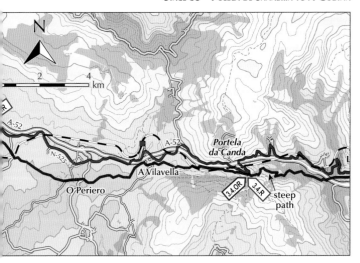

and leave the village on its southern side to join a dirt road after 400m. Follow the dirt road west passing underneath the motorway to a church, and join a path at its western end. Follow this path, often single track, with increasingly difficulty up the pass to the **Portela da Canda**, and the possibility of escaping onto the road route.

Leg 3.4.OR to O Canizo

Leg 3.4.OR does not involve any big climbs, but the stretches of single track will only appeal to cyclists who like a technical challenge.

From the pass, take a very steep descending gravel track down to a road and the settlement of A Canda. Follow the road for 1km and then leave it for a track on the left. The track passes underneath the railway to the village of **A Vilavella**. Go through the village to join a path on its southwest side. The path (occasionally track) follows the bottom of the valley, near a stream to **O Periero** (escape to the road route is possible here). Continue through the village and, as the road swings right, join a track, occasionally a path, through to a road. Follow the road for 300m, turn left onto a track and take this to **O Canizo**. The N-525 runs to the north of the village.

Leg 3.5.R to A Gudiña

Join the road and follow Leg 3.5.R as described in the road route.

A GUDIÑA

A Gudiña is a roadside Galician town that has lost its significance with the arrival of the motorway. There is nothing to see, but there are plenty of good-value hotels that also serve food. The Hotel Restaurante Suizo is clean, cheap and comfortable. Even cheaper pilgrimage-style accommodation can be found at the Albergue de Peregrinos da Gudiña (tel +34 988 59 40 06).

STAGE 4S

A Gudiña to Ourense

Start	A Gudiña
Distance	Road 97km, off-road 89km, hybrid 90km
Ascent	Road 1640m, off-road 1600m
Descent	Road 2460m, off-road 2430m
Time	Road 5hr 45min, off-road 7hr 20min, hybrid 6hr 40min
Hybrid route	Leg 4.1.R ➜ Leg 4.2.R ➜ Leg.4.3.R ➜ Leg 4.4.OR ➜ Leg 4.5.R ➜ Leg.4.6.R ➜ Leg 4.7.OR ➜ Leg.4.8.R ➜ Leg.4.9.R ➜ Leg 4.10.OR ➜ Leg 4.11.R

Stage 4 provides some of the best cycling on the Camino Sanabrés, but it's tough, with the recommended hybrid route taking more than six-and-a-half hours to complete. The cycling is excellent and varied, a lovely upland stretch to start with, then some long and interesting descents, followed by a big climb. The character of the cycling then changes as the route, following a big descent, leaves the mountains and enters a more undulating landscape with a maritime climate.

For once the road route is less direct than the off-road, 97km compared to 89km, and both routes are hilly. Navigation off-road on the last part of the journey, from Vilar de Gomareite, gets a little complicated and for this reason alone it might be preferable to stay on the road route.

For off-roaders the recommended hybrid route makes the day manageable. It avoids a short but difficult descent into Campobecerros and a lengthy climb to the top of the day's big pass.

There are plenty of places to stop for refreshments, with Laza the obvious initial break point. Not to be missed is the bar at Albergueria with its shell-festooned walls, conveniently located at the top of the pass, and a very entertaining place.

Stage 4S (Sanabrés): A Gudiña to Ourense

▶ LEG 4.1.R
To off-road junction

16km	1hr	80m

▶ LEG 4.2.OR
To Campobecerros

4km	20min	-180m
CHALLENGING		Good

▶ LEG 4.2.R
To Campobecerros

5km	15min	-180m

▶ LEG 4.3.R
To off-road junction

4km	15min	50m

▶ LEG 4.4.OR
To Laza

10km	1hr 30min	-540m
DIFFICULT		Excellent

▶ LEG 4.4.R
To Laza

15km	45min	-540m

▶ LEG 4.5.R
To off-road junction

4km	15min	50m

▶ LEG 4.6.OR
To Allbergueria

8km	1hr 10min	460m
CHALLENGING		Good

▶ LEG 4.6.R
To Allbergueria

8km	40min	460m

▶ LEG 4.7.OR
To junction with road

4km	20min	-30m
DIFFICULT		Good

▶ LEG 4.7.R
To junction with off-road

4km	15min	-30m

▶ LEG 4.8.R
To Vilar de Barrio

4km	15min	-260m

▶ LEG 4.8.OR
To Vilar de Barrio

4km	20min	-260m
CHALLENGING		Poor

▶ LEG 4.9.R
To Vilar de Gomareite

3km	15min	0m

▶ LEG 4.10.OR
To Xunqueria de Ambía

10km	45min	-120m
MODERATE		Good

▶ LEG 4.10.R
To Xunqueria de Ambía

12km	40min	-120m

▶ LEG 4.11.R
To Ourense

22km	1hr 10min	-330m

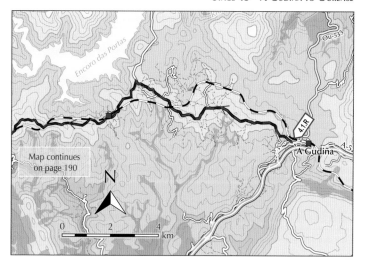

ROAD ROUTE

Leg 4.1.R to off-road junction

Leave the N-525 at the junction near the church in the centre of town and head northwest. After 8km, turn left at a junction and continue west for another 8km. As the road starts to descend, a Camino sign points out the off-road route.

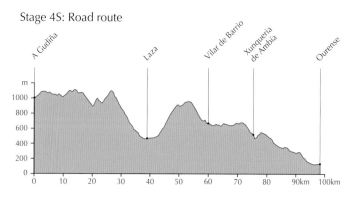

Stage 4S: Road route

Leg 4.2.R to Campobecerros
Follow a descending road down the side of the valley to **Campobecerros**, enjoying excellent views to the north.

Leg 4.3.R to off-road junction
Take the road west out of Campobecerros and follow an undulating road route for 4km, through the village of **Portocamba**, to the junction with the off-road route.

Leg 4.4.R to Laza
Go north at the junction and, after an initial climb, follow the road north around the head of the valley to **Cerdedelo**. Turn left onto a larger road and follow it down to **Laza**. At time of writing, construction traffic for the TGV had damaged the road at the head of the valley, but the surface has now been restored.

Leg 4.5.R to off-road junction
From Laza follow the road northwest along the valley, turn left after 1km and continue through the village of **Soutelo Verde**. The junction for the off-road route is about 400m north of the village.

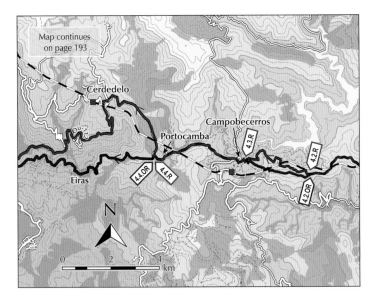

Scallop shells in the albergue at Albergueria

Leg 4.6.R to Allbergueria

Follow the road to **Allbergueria**, ignoring a left turn at a junction reached about halfway to the pass.

Leg 4.7.R to junction with off-road

From the bar in the centre of Allbergueria turn right and join the main road running north. Ignore a turn to the right and continue over the pass.

Leg 4.8.R to Vilar de Barrio

Go downhill from the junction, then continue, ignoring turns to left and right, to **Vilar de Barrio**.

Leg 4.9.R to Vilar de Gomareite

Cycle through Vilar de Barrio and bear left at a junction. Go through **Bóveda de Limia** and onto **Vilar de Gomareite**. For the off-road route, leave the road as it swings north.

Leg 4.10.R to Xunqueria de Ambía

From Vilar de Gomareite continue north, take a left turn at a junction, and continue to **Ponouzos**. Ignoring two turns on the right and then one on the left, head through **Busteliño** and **Bobadela**. Taking the second right after Bobadela, go through **Abeleda**, **Cima de Vila**, **Quintela** and, after taking a right turn, onto **Xunqueria de Ambía**.

Leg 4.11.R to Ourense

From Xunqueria de Ambía follow the road north across a bridge, take the first right and, ignoring left and right turns, continue for 6km, and head west into **Ousende** after crossing a railway. Continue west for another 5km to industrial **Reboredo**, reached after crossing another railway. Turn left onto a busy road, continue over a roundabout, past a major junction, and right onto another busy road. Follow this road through to **Ourense**.

OFF-ROAD (CAMINO) ROUTE

Leg 4.1.R to off-road junction

Follow Leg 4.1.R as described in the road route.

Leg 4.2.OR to Campobecerros

Leave the road, follow a track westwards along a ridge. After 2km the route starts a steep stony descent to the road into **Campobecerros**.

Leg 4.3.R to off-road junction

Join the road and follow Leg 4.3.R as described in the road route.

Stage 4S: Off-road route

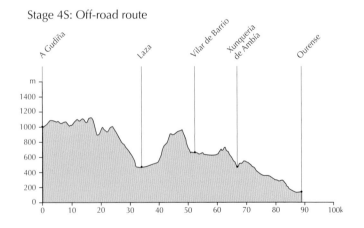

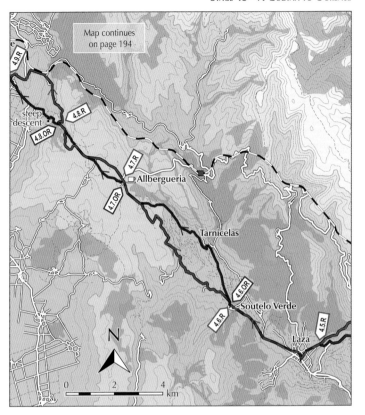

Leg 4.4.OR to Laza

Leg 4.4 is lovely, with great views north across the valley – the gravelly descent on the first half is tough and the road route again offers an excellent alternative.

Leave the road and join a southerly track across open, level ground. After about 1km, now heading west, the route enters trees and starts a steep descent to the village of **Eiras**. From Eiras follow a road for 4km to a turn-off onto a track, initially steep, that crosses the valley and joins a road heading into **Laza**. The turn-off is easily missed. If it is, continue on the road to a junction, and then turn right heading north into Laza.

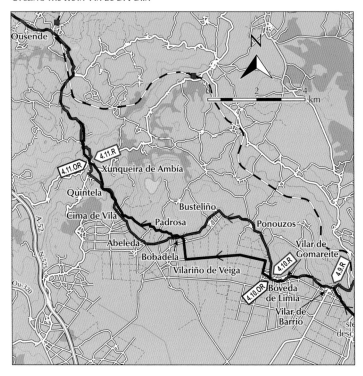

Leg 4.5.R to off-road junction
Join the road and follow Leg 4.5.R as described in the road route.

Leg 4.6.OR to Allbergueria
Take the track running along the valley bottom north to the small village of **Tarnicelas**. Go west from the church and join a track, initially heading south, and then northwest on a steep climb alongside the side of the valley. After a lot of walking – inevitable – join a road and follow it into **Allbergueria**.

Leg 4.7.OR to junction with road
From the bar in the centre of Allbergueria, turn left and head north through the village to a track, follow the track past a quarry, cross a road and, after running parallel with the main road from Allbergueria, cross it onto a track, and descend

194

for 1km to join the main road. Follow it for 600m and as the road swings right, the off-road turn-off is on the left.

Leg 4.8.OR to Vilar de Barrio
In 2018 the first part of this leg, the **steep descent**, had been washed away and was closed. If it has been reopened it goes directly downhill, descending 150m in a kilometre, turns left onto a road, leaves it after 300m to join a track, follows this to a road and then turns right into **Vilar de Barrio**. If the route has not been re-opened then follow the road route.

Leg 4.9.R to Vilar de Gomareite
Join the road and follow Leg 4.9.R as described in the road route.

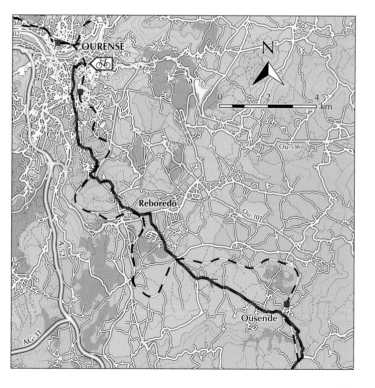

Leg 4.10.OR to Xunqueria de Ambía

If your legs are getting tired just do the first flat half of this off-road leg and join the road route at Bobadela; the second half of the route is both harder to follow and to cycle.

From the junction go through Vilar de Gomareite, turn right, head north for 300m and then turn left. Continue west along a flat agricultural track for 3km then turn right and continue north to Bobadela, crossing a road just before entering the village. Go through **Bobadela**, and then ascend onto a track heading through trees on its western side. After 1km cross a road, take the next left onto a road and follow it into **Padrosa**. Follow a track, sometimes a path, northwest for 3km to **Quintela** (crossing a road twice), turn right onto a track just past the village and continue to **Xunqueria de Ambía**.

Leg 4.11.OR to Ourense

Follow Leg 4.11.R as described in the road route.

OURENSE

Sitting astride the Miño River, Ourense (pop 107,000) is a vibrant city with a lovely centre. After several days in remote countryside, it's a good place to recharge your batteries.

The Romans founded the city, attracted to its location by thermal springs. It was laid waste by both Norse invasions and attacks from the Muslims and it wasn't until the 11th century that the city began to recover.

The most interesting part of the city is around the Plaza Mayor and the concentration of bars and restaurants to the north of cathedral. The San Martiño Cathedral is essentially Romanesque but includes Gothic, Renaissance, Baroque and even Neoclassical features. Also worth seeking out are two important Baroque churches, Santa María Nai (part of the Plaza Mayor), and Santa Eufemia. The town's most iconic structure is the Puente Mayor, the bridge over the Miño River. Originally Roman, the current elegant structure dates back to the 13th century.

There are lots of hotels in Ourense (note the parador is not located in the centre). The NH Ourense is good: very modern, with rooftop views over the city. Pilgrimage-style accommodation can be found at the municipal *albergue* (tel +34 608 868 434) or at a private *albergue* (tel +34 988 614 564) which, unlike the municipal version, has secure bike parking.

STAGE 5S

Ourense to Lalín or Lalín Station

Start	Ourense
Distance	Road 51km, off-road 57km
Ascent	Road 1160m, off-road 1350m
Descent	Road 780m, off-road 1010m
Time	Road 3hr 20min, off-road 4hr 45min
Hybrid route	Same as off-road route

It's about 100km from Ourense to Santiago de Compostela. Road cyclists, following the N-525 all the way, will probably prefer to do this in a day, particularly as there is very little to see in Lalín. For off-road or touring cyclists the decision will probably depend on the weather and personal preference as the route is good but not spectacular. The landscape in this part of Spain is very green, dominated by cows (Galicia produces most of Spain's milk), and reminiscent of the west of England. If the weather is good, and the ground reasonably dry, a two-day strategy makes sense. If it's wet, the tracks can be unpleasant, and with so many cows the puddles contain more than just water. In these conditions a more direct route to Santiago de Compostela should be considered.

The 51km road route blasts along the N-525 and could be completed in 3hr 20mins. The toughest part of the route (as with the off-road route) is the climb out of Ourense.

The off-road stage is 57km long and should take just under 5hr to complete. Although there are no big climbs, the route is distinctly undulating and gains 1420m against 1090m descent. The route is not direct and substituting the road route on Leg 4 and missing the visit to Oseira and its monastery would save at least an hour.

The off-road stage ends at Lalín Station, which has a choice of good value accommodation. Lalín is another 5km and going there will therefore also add another 5km to the following day's journey.

Stage 5S (Sanabrés): Ourense to Lalín or Lalín Station

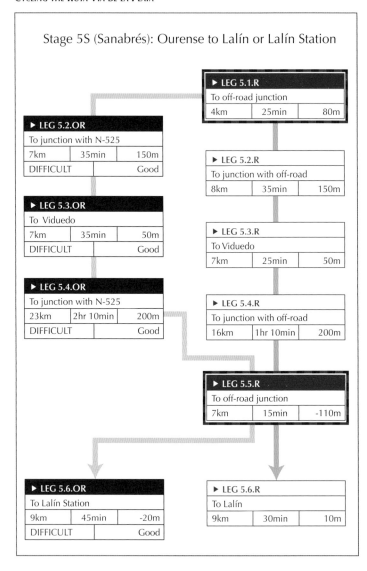

▶ LEG 5.1.R

To off-road junction

4km	25min	80m

▶ LEG 5.2.OR

To junction with N-525

7km	35min	150m
DIFFICULT		Good

▶ LEG 5.2.R

To junction with off-road

8km	35min	150m

▶ LEG 5.3.OR

To Viduedo

7km	35min	50m
DIFFICULT		Good

▶ LEG 5.3.R

To Viduedo

7km	25min	50m

▶ LEG 5.4.OR

To junction with N-525

23km	2hr 10min	200m
DIFFICULT		Good

▶ LEG 5.4.R

To junction with off-road

16km	1hr 10min	200m

▶ LEG 5.5.R

To off-road junction

7km	15min	-110m

▶ LEG 5.6.OR

To Lalín Station

9km	45min	-20m
DIFFICULT		Good

▶ LEG 5.6.R

To Lalín

9km	30min	10m

ROAD ROUTE

Leg 5.1.R to off-road junction

Starting from Parque de San Lázaro in the centre of Ourense, take the northern left-hand exit, head up to the main road, turn left and continue to a roundabout. Take the second exit and then the first right. Turn right again onto the Rue Pointe Romana and head down to Ourense's spectacular bridge. Cross the bridge and continue north to a one-way system (part of the N-525). Continue north along the N-525 for 1.5km, turning left at the first significant junction. Take the first right

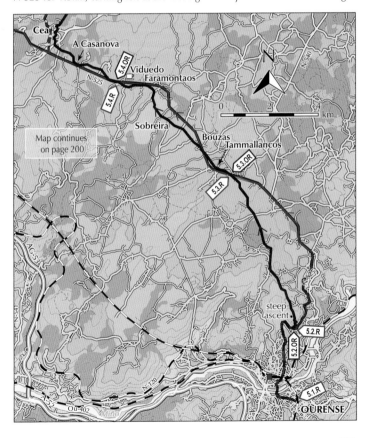

Stage 5S: Road route

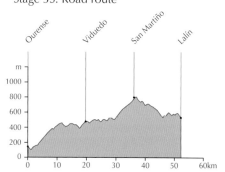

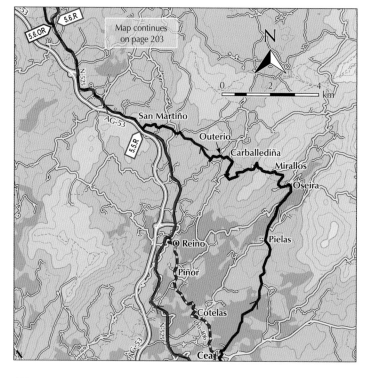

Map continues on page 203

and follow a road for another 2km as it swings around a valley. The off-road junction is in the middle of shops in front of a pedestrian crossing.

Leg 5.2.R to junction with off-road
From the junction with the off-road continue on the same road for another 4km, turn left onto the N-525 and continue to the off-road junction near the K251 marker.

Leg 5.3.R to Viduedo
Head west on the N-525 to Viduedo.

Leg 5.4.R to junction with off-road
Continue on the N-525 to **San Martiño**.

Variant via Cea and Piñor
If the N-525 has at this point become just too tedious, turn off after 4km and head into **Cea**. From Cea take the OU-406 to **Cotelas**, through **Piñor** and then back onto the N-525 near **O Reino**.

Leg 5.5.R to off-road junction
Follow a gently descending route for 7km to the junction with the off-road route. The junction can be found near tall trees on the brow of a hill.

Leg 5.6.R to Lalín
Continue on the N-525 into **Lalín**.

> There is lots of choice for accommodation in **Lalín** itself, and the Hotel Restaurante El Palacio comes highly recommended.

OFF-ROAD (CAMINO) ROUTE

Leg 5.1.R to off-road junction
Follow Leg 5.1.R as described in the road route.

Leg 5.2.OR to junction with N-525
The first part of the off-road leg involves a steep climb.

Head north along a road, then track, taking a sharp left turn after 400m past a church (above the track) and continue for 3km to a road. Turn right onto the road and after a few metres join a track on the right. Turn left after 1km and continue north for around 4km to the N-525.

Green Galicia

Stage 5S: Off-road route

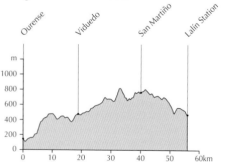

Leg 5.3.OR to Viduedo

This short leg switches from the north side of the N-525 to south side and then rejoins it at Viduedo: for a simple life stay on the N-525.

Crossing the N-525 join a small road to the village

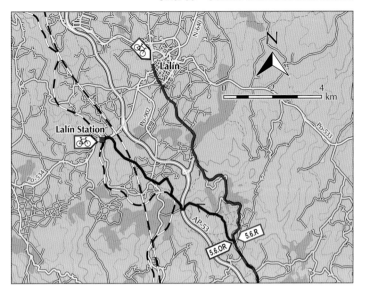

of **Tammallancos** and onto **Bouzas**. Cross the N-525 again and follow a road/track through **Sobreira**, turn left and immediately right and head down a track to a medieval bridge. Cross the bridge and climb a sticky track up to and through the village of **Faramontaos** and onto **Viduedo**, where refreshments can be found.

Leg 5.4.OR to junction with N-525

From Viduedo the route goes north on some occasionally challenging terrain to Oseira and its monastery. There is nothing to see at the monastery apart from its austere exterior. If the weather is poor there will be wet muddy stretches made worse by the cattle.

Join a track on the right-hand side of the N-525 just on from Viduedo and follow it through **A Casanova** and up to the small town of **Cea**. Head north through the town to a football pitch and turn right on its northern side. Turn left and, after a couple of buildings, leave the road to join a track. Follow the track north through trees for 3km, emerging on a road/occasional track before joining a proper road 3km later at **Pielas**. Turn right and continue to **Oseira**.

Turn left at the Café Bar Venezuela and, ignoring Camino signs, continue west for 300m before turning right and climbing steeply up the side of the valley to the little settlement of **Mirallos**. Turn left, continue downhill for 3km and turn right at a junction. Follow the road to the village of **Carballediña**, turn left (picking up the Camino signs again) and continue for 1km to the village of **Outerio**. Continue for 3km along a track before bearing right to rejoin the N-525 at **San Martiño**.

Leg 5.5.R to off-road junction
Follow Leg 5.5.R as described in the road route.

Leg 5.6.OR to Lalín Station
This short stage has some steep descents that, depending on the weather, can be challenging.

Follow a descending track and bear left at a fork, passing over the motorway and down to a narrow road. The descent at times is steep. Turn left off the road onto a narrow gravel track (in bad weather continue on the road and turn left at the top of the hill) climbing up to a junction. Turn right onto a small road and follow it over a hill and down to **Lalín Station**.

LALÍN STATION

There are three small hotels at Lalín Station and the Restaurante Hostal A Taberna De Vento features on Booking.com. The author stayed at the hotel opposite, and found them particularly kind when he turned up wet and muddy and in a rainstorm. Unfortunately, details are not available and the hotel does not have an obvious web presence.

STAGE 6S

Lalín to Santiago de Compostela

Start	Lalín or Lalín Station
Distance	Road 50km, off-road 55km
Ascent	Road 780m, off-road 1110m
Descent	Road 1050m, off-road 1320m
Time	Road 3hr 20min, off-road 4hr 50min
Hybrid route	Same as off-road route

Although Stage 6 is short, 50km on road and 55km for off-road, there are still some off-road challenges to overcome before it's time to celebrate the end of the trip. Although generally not that hilly, the landscape is deeply incised by rivers, with steep descents and ascents. The off-road route will take about 4hr 50min to complete, gains some 1200m and loses 1400m. The road route tends to cross the river gorges in a more civilised way and gains only 830m while losing 1100m, so it should be possible to get to Santiago de Compostela in less than three and a half hours.

The landscape is similar to Stage 5 to begin with, but gets progressively more urban on the approach to the city. The road and off-road routes are never that far apart, and while the off-road follows tracks and small roads, it no longer has the remote feel of the earlier stages.

There are plenty of places to stop for a break, but Ponte Ulla on the off-road route is perhaps the prettiest.

ROAD ROUTE

Leg 6.1.R to Prado
Continue on the N-525 to **Prado,** where the off-road and road routes meet again after their separation before Lalín.

Leg 6.2.R to Silleda
Continue on the N-525 to **Silleda**.

Stage 6S (Sanabrés): Lalín to Santiago de Compostela

▶ LEG 6.1.OR		
To Prado		
8km	40min	-40m
MODERATE		Good

▶ LEG 6.1.R		
To Prado		
7km	25min	-100m

▶ LEG 6.2.OR		
To Silleda		
7km	30min	40m
MODERATE		Good

▶ LEG 6.2.R		
To Silleda		
6km	25min	40m

▶ LEG 6.3.OR		
To Bandeira		
6km	40min	-60m
DIFFICULT		Good

▶ LEG 6.3.R		
To Bandeira		
6km	40min	-60m

▶ LEG 6.4.OR		
To Ponte Ulla		
13km	1hr 10min	-360m
DIFFICULT		Good

▶ LEG 6.4.R		
To Ponte Ulla		
12km	45min	-310m

▶ LEG 6.5.OR		
To junction with N-525		
11km	55min	110m
MODERATE		Good

▶ LEG 6.5.R		
To junction with off-road		
10km	30min	110m

▶ LEG 6.6.R		
To off-road junction		
3km	10min	-20m

▶ LEG 6.7.OR		
To Santiago de Compostela		
7km	35min	70m
MODERATE		Poor

▶ LEG 6.7.R		
To Santiago de Compostela		
6km	25min	70m

Stage 6S: Road route

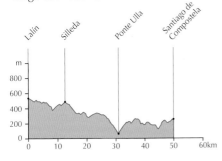

Leg 6.3.R to Bandeira
Continue on the N-525 to **Bandeira**.

Leg 6.4.R to Ponte Ulla
Continue on the N-525 to just beyond **Ponte Ulla**. A flyover takes the hard work out of the gorge and connects with the off-road route just beyond the village.

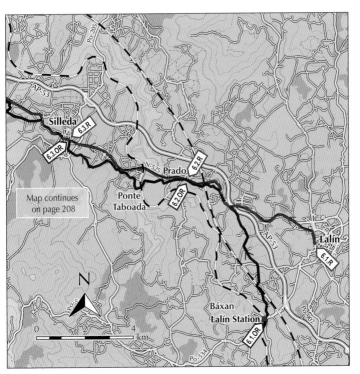

207

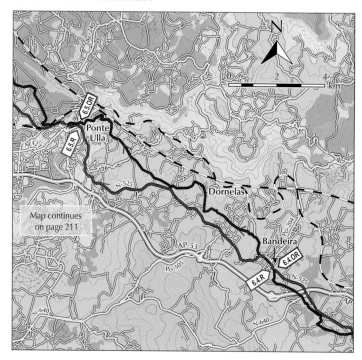

Leg 6.5.R to junction with off-road

Continue with the N-525 to the junction with the off-road.

Leg 6.6.R to off-road junction

Continue on the N-525 for 3km and take a right turn just after the K334 kilometre marker.

Stage 6S: Off-road route

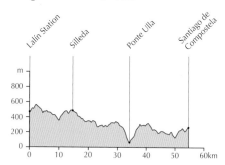

Leg 6.7.R to Santiago de Compostela

Continue on the N-525 into the city. After passing beneath the railway, cross a roundabout, turn right at the next roundabout, and head into the historic city centre of **Santiago de Compostela**.

OFF-ROAD (CAMINO) ROUTE

Leg 6.1.OR to Prado

Head east from the roundabout near Lalín Station, take the first left and continue to **Báxan**. Continue north (ignoring Camino markers), take a right turn over the railway and, after turning left (the Camino markers return) continue to a road. Cross the road and join a track, take a right turn after 500m and a left turn 500m later. Continue to the N-525 and follow it before turning left onto a track after 800m and heading into **Prado**.

Leg 6.2.OR to Silleda

The off-road route stays on the N-525 for a few metres then turns onto a track running immediately behind roadside houses. Follow the track west into trees to descend beneath a railway, across a lovely old bridge (**Ponte Taboada**) and up a steep hill to a small village. Continue up the hill on a small road, cross it onto a track and head up to the N-525. Without actually going on the N-525 swing left and follow a track westwards over a road into **Silleda**.

Leg 6.3.OR to Bandeira

Follow the N-525 for 1.5km before joining a track on the left, continue for 1.5km (ignoring the Camino markers), turn right at a junction, and left 300m later (Camino markers should return). Follow a road heading beneath the N-525 and over the motorway, turning right at a junction 1km later. Follow this road up to the N-525 and into **Bandeira**.

Leg 6.4.OR to Ponte Ulla

Continue through Bandeira and turn right onto a smaller road as the N-525 swings left. Continue on this road for 2.5km, ignoring turns off it, and crossing a junction with a road, join a smaller road/track. Turn right onto a road after 1.5km, follow through the small village of **Dornelas**. Turn left at a junction and after 1km left again, joining a road heading back to the N-525. Before reaching the N-525, turn right onto a track and follow it northwest, crossing a road after 2km. Continue along what is now a small road, through a series of settlements, before descending to **Ponte Ulla**.

Leg 6.5.OR to junction with N-525

Cross the old bridge and join a steep road/track climbing up to the N-525. Continue climbing on the N-525 for 800m and then take a sharp right turn. Turn left after 50m onto a track, then left again before turning right onto a road. Turn right again and, after 300m take a left turn onto a forest track. Follow this track for 4km to a junction with a road. Turn left and follow the road for 500m; then leave it to join a track as the road turns south. Follow the track for 2km, turn left onto a road and, after crossing one junction, turn right and head into the village of **Rubial**. Turn left at the junction in the village and follow a road to the village of **Deseiro de Abraixo**. Ignoring Camino markers, follow the road just beyond the village to the N-525.

Leg 6.6.R to off-road junction

Join the road and follow Leg 6.6.R as described in the road route.

Leg 6.7.OR to Santiago de Compostela

The final leg is a little disappointing – a messy route through the city's urban fringe.

From the turn-off follow the road for 300m and turn left before the railway bridge. Follow this road as it swings left and over a junction. Take the next right and then the next left. Continue west and, after crossing a river and a bigger road, join a track and pass underneath the motorway. After 100m turn left onto a road then right over a railway bedecked with items left by pilgrims. Take the next right and then immediate left; continue on this road into the centre of **Santiago de Compostela**.

Discarded pilgrims clothing on the way into Santiago de Compostella

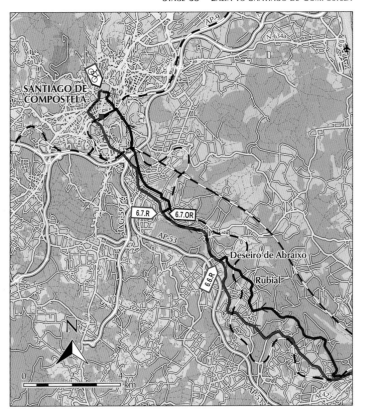

SANTIAGO DE COMPOSTELA

Santiago de Compostela (96,000) is a remarkable place. Full of pilgrims coming to the end of their labours, it takes a little time to get under that surface and find the city that works for its own inhabitants as well.

The city owes its origins to the discovery of the remains of St James by a local shepherd, a discovery which was promptly ratified by the Bishop who passed on the good news to King Alfonso II in Oviedo. The cathedral was built on the spot where the remains are said to have been found, and

Facade of the Cathedral of Santiago de Compostela (photo: Sandy Brown)

pilgrims began arriving to what by the 10th century was the most important Christian pilgrimage destination after Rome and Jerusalem.

Gathering in the cathedral to watch the Botafumeiro, smoking with incense and swinging from its pulley, is the highlight of many pilgrims' visit to the city and the cathedral is an impressive if crowded heart to an impressive medieval centre. The current cathedral has a Romanesque core, but most of the façades were built later and are Baroque in character. On the western side is the magnificent Praza do Obradoiro, the main square of the old town and the place to get an end of trip picture. The northern side of the square is formed by Hostal dos Reis Católicos, built by Ferdinand and Isabel, now a parador and the oldest operating hotel in the world.

The medieval core of the city can be very lively place and, in the narrow alleys to the north locals co-mingle with pilgrims and keep the bars and restaurants busy. The food in Santiago de Compostela is really good, particularly the seafood. For Michelin star tapas try the Abastos 2 located near the market although my favourite restaurant, and cheaper, is Curro da Parra.

If the parador is a little grand there are plenty of less ostentatious alternatives. Well located is Pousadas de Compostela. For pilgrimage-style, consider the enormous Albergue Seminario Menor (177 places, tel +34 981 589 200) or one many private albergues including the Albergue Acuario (tel +34 981 575 438).

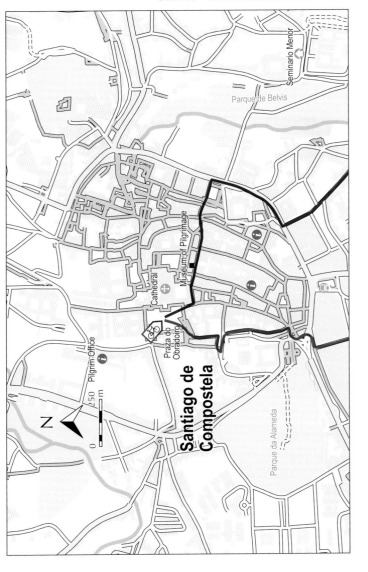

APPENDIX A
Accommodation

This is a selection of accommodation available at the end of stages or alternative ends of stages. Web address are provided if not on Booking.com, www.booking.com.

Price ranges are as follows
€€€ = €80–110 (twin room)
€€ = €40–80 (twin room)
€ = pilgrimage-style accommodation up to €30

Seville
Las Casas de la Juderia €€€
Upmarket, great location
tel +34 954 41 51 50

Hotel San Gil €€€
Well located for restaurants
tel +34 954 90 68 11

Pension Doña Trinidad €€
Good location, great value
tel +34 954 54 19 06

Albergue Triana €
Good reviews, but located on the west side of the river
tel +34 954 45 99 60

Almadén de la Plata
Hotel El Romeral €€
Best restaurant
tel +34 954 73 54 53

Hostal Restaurante Casa Concha €€
tel +34 954 73 50 43

Municipal albergue €
tel +34 692 735 043

El Real de la Jara
Hostal La Encina €€
tel +34 625 99 83 00

Alojamiento Mo Carmen €€
Primitive, but near the restaurant
tel +34 647 07 87 41

Municipal albergue €
tel +34 954 733 007

Or a private albergue
tel +34 654 862 553

Zafra
Parador de Zafra €€€
Zafra's original castle
tel +34 924 55 45 40

Casa Palacio Conde de la Corte Hotel €€€
Favoured by bullfighters
tel +34 924 56 33 11

Hotel Adarve €€
Built into the city walls
tel +34 619 19 84 94

San Francisco Convent Hostel €
tel +34 691 53 72 83

Mérida
Parador de Mérida €€€
Located in a former convent
tel +34 924 31 38 00

Mérida Palace €€€
Parador style but with a rooftop swimming pool
tel +34 924 38 38 00

Hostal Emeritae €€
Good value, good location
tel +34 924 30 31 83

Albergue de Peregrinos, Molino de Pan
Caliente €
tel +34 682 51 43 66

Cáceres
Parador de Cáceres €€€
A beautiful Renaissance palace
tel +34 927 21 17 59

Palacio de Oquendo €€€
Another great location
tel +34 927 21 58 00

Hotel Albarragena €€
Good value
tel +34 927 03 72 95

El Albergue Ciudad de Cáceres €
tel +34 927 24 97 68

Casar de Cáceres
Albergue Turistico
Ruta de la Plata de Cesar €€
tel +34 927 291 193

Grimaldo
La Posada de Grimaldo €€
A *casa rural*
tel +34 616 93 17 45

Albergue municipal €
tel +34 645 125 102

Carcaboso
Hostal Ciudad de Cáparra €€
Excellent value
tel +34 927 40 24 44

Plasencia
Parador de Plasencia €€€
In the 15th-century Santo Domingo
Monastery
tel +34 927 42 58 70

Hotel Palacio Carvajal Girón €€€
In a stunningly converted Renaissance
palace
tel +34 927 42 63 26

Hotel Exe Alfonso VIII €€
Good location, good value
tel +34 927 41 02 50

Albergue Santa Ana €
tel +34 927 41 02 88

Baños de Montemayor
Hostal las Termas €€
Near the spa
tel +34 927 48 83 20

Albergue Vía de la Plata €
tel +34 655 620 515

Béjar
Hotel Colón €€
Best of a limited choice
tel +34 923 40 06 50

Salamanca
Palacio de Castellanos €€€
Potentially expensive
tel +34 923 26 18 18

Hospes Palacio de San Esteban €€€€
Another lovely building, potentially
expensive
tel +34 923 26 22 96

Hostal Plaza Mayor €€
Great location, but some rooms are
noisy
tel +34 923 26 20 20

Casa la Calera €
tel +34 652 921 185

Zamora
Parador de Zamora €€€
Located in a 15th-century palace
tel +34 980 51 44 97

215

Zamora Palacio del Duoroz €€€
A restored industrial building
tel +34 980 50 82 62

San Gil Plaza €€
Apartment-style hotel
tel +34 980 04 84 70

Albergue de Peregrinos €
tel +34 980 50 94 27

Benavente
Parador de Benavente €€€
Featuring a 15th-century castle tower
tel +34 980 63 03 00

La Trapería Pensión €€
Great location
tel +34 650 58 62 11

Albergue Municipal de Peregrinos €
tel +34 980 63 42 11

León
Parador de León €€€
Arguably the best parador in the world
tel +34 987 23 73 00

Hotel Vía León €€
Great location
tel +34 987 03 54 81

Municipal Albergue €
tel +34 987 081 832

Pola de Lena
Hotel Ruta de la Plata €€
Good value
tel +34 985 49 77 01

Albergue de Peregrinosi €
tel +34 985 49 22 47

Oviedo
Hotel de la Reconquista €€€
18th-century palace
tel +34 985 24 11 00

Ayre Hotel Ramiro I €€
Just south of the centre
tel +34 985 23 28 50

Albergue de Peregrinos de Oviedo €
tel +34 985 22 85 25

Albergue Turistico La Peregrina €
tel +34 687 13 39 32

Gijón
Parador de Gijón €€€
Located in a park to the east of the
city centre
tel +34 985 37 05 11

Hotel Marqués €€
Located near the marina
tel +34 985 09 09 29

Albergue Merendero El Peregrin €
Pilgrimage-style accommodation
tel +34 652 76 76 01

Tábara
Hotel El Roble €€
Good value
elrobletabara@gmail.com

Municipal albergue €
tel +34 637 926 068

Puebla de Sanabria
Posada de las Misas €€
Excellent, and with the town's best
restaurant
tel +34 980 62 03 58

Casa Luz €
Summer months only
www.alberguecasaluz.es

A Gudiña
Hotel Restaurante Suizo €€
One of several good-value hotels
tel +34 988 42 10 66

Albergue de Peregrinos da Gudiña €
tel +34 988 59 40 06

Ourense
NH Ourense €€€
Very modern with rooftop views
tel +34 988 60 11 11

Hotel Zarampalla €€
Good location
tel +34 988 23 00 08

Municipal albergue €
tel +34 608 868 434

Lalín
Hotel Restaurante El Palacio €
tel +34 986 78 00 00

Lalín Station
Restaurante Hostal A Taberna
De Vento €€
tel +34 986 78 07 34

Santiago de Compostela
Pousadas de Compostela €€
Well located
tel +34 981 56 93 50

Albergue Seminario Menor €
tel +34 981 589 200
(177 places)

APPENDIX B
Useful contacts

Airlines

British Airways www.britishairways.com

easyJet www.easyjet.com

Iberia www.iberia.com

Ryanair www.ryanair.com

Vueling www.vueling.com

Train travel
Seat61 www.seat61.com

Coach travel
ALSA www.alsa.com

Tourist and pilgrim information

The Association of the Ruta Vía de la
Plata www.rutadelaplata.com/

The Spanish Tourist Board
www.spain.info/

Camino de Santiago
http://santiago-compostela.net/
Information on pilgrim routes to
Santiago de Compostela

Bike hire
bikeiberia Bike Tours & Rentals
www.bikeiberia.com

Bike transport service from the UK
SendBike www.sendbike.com

Bike transport service from Spain
Velocipedo www.elvelocipedo.com

Central Parador (booking service with
pilgrim discounts available)
https://www.parador.es/

APPENDIX C
Spanish-English glossary

Spanish	English
acequia	water channel
alameda	park or promenade in town centre
alberca	water tank
albergue	hostel
alcázar	fortress
alquería	from the Arab al-qairia: a mountain farm or hamlet
arroyo	stream
ayuntamiento	town hall
barranco	gulley or gorge
barrio	district /quarter of town or village
calera	lime kiln
calzada	footpath, originally cobbled
cañada/colada/cordel	drovers' track or transhumance route
capilla	chapel
casa cueva	cave house
castillo	castle
cerro	hill or low mountain
consultorio	doctor's surgery
cordillera	mountain range

Spanish	English
cortijo	farmhouse/farm
coto	hunting reserve
dehesa	forest that has been partially cleared to leave select species such as evergreen, deciduous and cork oak
embalse	reservoir
era	threshing floor
ermita	chapel
espeleología	caving
frontera	border
fuente	spring
ganadería	livestock
huerta/huerto	cultivated plot where fruit and veg are grown
lavandería	wash house
llano	plain, flat extension between mountains
majanos	piles of stones
mesón	restaurant
mirador	viewpoint
molino	mill
monte bajo	low growing, shrubby vegetation

Spanish	English
morisco	Muslims who adopted the Christian faith
nacimiento	source of spring, river or stream
nava	flat area between outcrops of rock
pantano	reservoir
parador	a hotel group owned and managed by the state
paseo	park or promenade in town centre
puerto	pass
prohidido el paso	no entry
ración	whole plate of any particular tapas
rambla	causeway of river, often dry, synonymous with wadi

Spanish	English
rió	river
sendero	footpath
sierra	mountain range (less extensive than cordillera)
taha	district
tajo	gorge or cliff face
tapa	small saucer/dish of food to accompany drink
tinao	roof or room spanning street in Las Alpujarras
venta	restaurant
vereda	footpath
vía verde	former railway line converted to walk/cycle path

DOWNLOAD THE ROUTES
IN GPX FORMAT

All the routes in this guide are available for download from:

www.cicerone.co.uk/1012/GPX

as standard format GPX files. You should be able to load them into most online GPX systems and mobile devices, whether GPS or smartphone. You may need to convert the file into your preferred format using a conversion programme such as gpsvisualizer.com or one of the many other such websites and programmes.

When you follow this link, you will be asked for your email address and where you purchased the guidebook, and have the option to subscribe to the Cicerone e-newsletter.

www.cicerone.co.uk

LISTING OF CICERONE GUIDES

BRITISH ISLES CHALLENGES, COLLECTIONS AND ACTIVITIES

Cycling Land's End to John o' Groats
The Big Rounds
The Book of the Bivvy
The Book of the Bothy
The Mountains of England & Wales:
    Vol 1 Wales
    Vol 2 England
The National Trails
Walking The End to End Trail

SCOTLAND

Ben Nevis and Glen Coe
Cycle Touring in Northern Scotland
Cycling in the Hebrides
Great Mountain Days in Scotland
Mountain Biking in Southern and
    Central Scotland
Mountain Biking in West and North
    West Scotland
Not the West Highland Way
Scotland
Scotland's Best Small Mountains
Scotland's Mountain Ridges
Skye's Cuillin Ridge Traverse
The Borders Abbeys Way
The Great Glen Way
The Great Glen Way Map Booklet
The Hebridean Way
The Hebrides
The Isle of Mull
The Isle of Skye
The Skye Trail
The Southern Upland Way
The Speyside Way
The Speyside Way Map Booklet
The West Highland Way
The West Highland Way
    Map Booklet
Walking Ben Lawers, Rannoch
    and Atholl
Walking in the Cairngorms
Walking in the Pentland Hills
Walking in the Scottish Borders
Walking in the Southern Uplands
Walking in Torridon
Walking Loch Lomond and
    the Trossachs
Walking on Arran
Walking on Harris and Lewis
Walking on Jura, Islay and Colonsay
Walking on Rum and the Small Isles
Walking on the Orkney and
    Shetland Isles
Walking on Uist and Barra
Walking the Cape Wrath Trail
Walking the Corbetts
    Vol 1 South of the Great Glen
    Vol 2 North of the Great Glen

Walking the Galloway Hills
Walking the Munros
    Vol 1 – Southern, Central and
        Western Highlands
    Vol 2 – Northern Highlands and
        the Cairngorms
Winter Climbs Ben Nevis and
    Glen Coe
Winter Climbs in the Cairngorms

NORTHERN ENGLAND ROUTES

Cycling the Reivers Route
Cycling the Way of the Roses
Hadrian's Cycleway
Hadrian's Wall Path
Hadrian's Wall Path Map Booklet
The C2C Cycle Route
The Pennine Way
The Pennine Way Map Booklet
The Coast to Coast Walk
The Coast to Coast Map Booklet
Walking the Dales Way
Walking the Dales Way Map Booklet

NORTH EAST ENGLAND, YORKSHIRE DALES AND PENNINES

Cycling in the Yorkshire Dales
Great Mountain Days in
    the Pennines
Mountain Biking in the
    Yorkshire Dales
St Oswald's Way and
    St Cuthbert's Way
The Cleveland Way and the
    Yorkshire Wolds Way
The Cleveland Way Map Booklet
The North York Moors
The Reivers Way
The Teesdale Way
Trail and Fell Running in the
    Yorkshire Dales
Walking in County Durham
Walking in Northumberland
Walking in the North Pennines
Walking in the Yorkshire Dales:
    North and East
Walking in the Yorkshire Dales:
    South and West

NORTH WEST ENGLAND AND THE ISLE OF MAN

Cycling the Pennine Bridleway
Isle of Man Coastal Path
The Lancashire Cycleway
The Lune Valley and Howgills
Walking in Cumbria's Eden Valley
Walking in Lancashire
Walking in the Forest of Bowland
    and Pendle

Walking on the Isle of Man
Walking on the West Pennine Moors
Walks in Silverdale and Arnside

LAKE DISTRICT

Cycling in the Lake District
Great Mountain Days in the
    Lake District
Joss Naylor's Lakes, Meres and
    Waters of the Lake District
Lake District Winter Climbs
Lake District: High Level and
    Fell Walks
Lake District: Low Level and
    Lake Walks
Mountain Biking in the Lake District
Outdoor Adventures with Children –
    Lake District
Scrambles in the Lake District –
    North
Scrambles in the Lake District –
    South
The Cumbria Way
Trail and Fell Running in the
    Lake District
Walking the Lake District Fells –
    Borrowdale
    Buttermere
    Coniston
    Keswick
    Langdale
    Mardale and the Far East
    Patterdale
    Wasdale
Walking the Tour of the Lake District

DERBYSHIRE, PEAK DISTRICT AND MIDLANDS

Cycling in the Peak District
Dark Peak Walks
Scrambles in the Dark Peak
Walking in Derbyshire
Walking in the Peak District –
    White Peak East
Walking in the Peak District –
    White Peak West

SOUTHERN ENGLAND

20 Classic Sportive Rides in
    South East England
20 Classic Sportive Rides in
    South West England
Cycling in the Cotswolds
Mountain Biking on the
    North Downs
Mountain Biking on the
    South Downs
Walking the South West Coast Path
South West Coast Path Map Booklets
    Vol 1: Minehead to St Ives
    Vol 2: St Ives to Plymouth
    Vol 3: Plymouth to Poole

Suffolk Coast and Heath Walks
The Cotswold Way
The Cotswold Way Map Booklet
The Great Stones Way
The Kennet and Avon Canal
The Lea Valley Walk
The North Downs Way
The North Downs Way Map Booklet
The Peddars Way and Norfolk
   Coast path
The Pilgrims' Way
The Ridgeway National Trail
The Ridgeway Map Booklet
The South Downs Way
The South Downs Way Map Booklet
The Thames Path
The Thames Path Map Booklet
The Two Moors Way
The Two Moors Way Map Booklet
Walking Hampshire's Test Way
Walking in Cornwall
Walking in Essex
Walking in Kent
Walking in London
Walking in Norfolk
Walking in the Chilterns
Walking in the Cotswolds
Walking in the Isles of Scilly
Walking in the New Forest
Walking in the North Wessex Downs
Walking on Dartmoor
Walking on Guernsey
Walking on Jersey
Walking on the Isle of Wight
Walking the Jurassic Coast
Walks in the South Downs
   National Park

WALES AND WELSH BORDERS

Cycle Touring in Wales
Cycling Lon Las Cymru
Glyndwr's Way
Great Mountain Days in Snowdonia
Hillwalking in Shropshire
Hillwalking in Wales – Vols 1&2
Mountain Walking in Snowdonia
Offa's Dyke Path
Offa's Dyke Map Booklet
Ridges of Snowdonia
Scrambles in Snowdonia
Snowdonia: 30 Low-level and easy
   walks – North
Snowdonia: 30 Low-level and easy
   walks – South
The Cambrian Way
The Ceredigion and Snowdonia
   Coast Paths
The Pembrokeshire Coast Path
The Pembrokeshire Coast Path
   Map Booklet
The Severn Way

The Snowdonia Way
The Wales Coast Path
The Wye Valley Walk
Walking in Carmarthenshire
Walking in Pembrokeshire
Walking in the Forest of Dean
Walking in the Wye Valley
Walking on Gower
Walking on the Brecon Beacons
Walking the Shropshire Way

INTERNATIONAL CHALLENGES, COLLECTIONS AND ACTIVITIES

Canyoning in the Alps
Europe's High Points

ALPS CROSS-BORDER ROUTES

100 Hut Walks in the Alps
Alpine Ski Mountaineering
   Vol 1 – Western Alps
   Vol 2 – Central and Eastern Alps
Chamonix to Zermatt
The Karnischer Hohenweg
The Tour of the Bernina
Tour of Monte Rosa
Tour of the Matterhorn
Trail Running – Chamonix and the
   Mont Blanc region
Trekking in the Alps
Trekking in the Silvretta and
   Ratikon Alps
Trekking Munich to Venice
Trekking the Tour of Mont Blanc
Walking in the Alps

AFRICA

Walking in the Drakensberg
KilimanjaroThe High Atlas
Walks and Scrambles in the
   Moroccan Anti-Atlas

PYRENEES AND FRANCE/SPAIN CROSS-BORDER ROUTES

Shorter Treks in the Pyrenees
The GR10 Trail
The GR11 Trail
The Pyrenean Haute Route
The Pyrenees
Walks and Climbs in the Pyrenees

AUSTRIA

Innsbruck Mountain Adventures
The Adlerweg
Trekking in Austria's Hohe Tauern
Trekking in the Stubai Alps
Trekking in the Zillertal Alps
Walking in Austria
Walking in the Salzkammergut:
   the Austrian Lake District

EASTERN EUROPE

The Danube Cycleway Vol 2
The Elbe Cycle Route
The High Tatras
The Mountains of Romania
Walking in Bulgaria's National Parks
Walking in Hungary

FRANCE, BELGIUM AND LUXEMBOURG

Chamonix Mountain Adventures
Cycle Touring in France
Cycling London to Paris
Cycling the Canal de la Garonne
Cycling the Canal du Midi
Mont Blanc Walks
Mountain Adventures in
   the Maurienne
Short Treks on Corsica
The GR20 Corsica
The GR5 Trail
The GR5 Trail – Benelux
   and Lorraine
The GR5 Trail – Vosges and Jura
The Grand Traverse of the
   Massif Central
The Loire Cycle Route
The Moselle Cycle Route
The River Rhone Cycle Route
The Way of St James – Le Puy to
   the Pyrenees
Tour of the Queyras
Trekking in the Vanoise
Trekking the Cathar Way
Trekking the Robert Louis
   Stevenson Trail
Vanoise Ski Touring
Via Ferratas of the French Alps
Walking in Provence – East
Walking in Provence – West
Walking in the Ardennes
Walking in the Auvergne
Walking in the Briannconnais
Walking in the Dordogne
Walking in the Haute Savoie: North
Walking in the Haute Savoie: South
Walking on Corsica

GERMANY

Hiking and Cycling in the
   Black Forest
The Danube Cycleway Vol 1
The Rhine Cycle Route
The Westweg
Walking in the Bavarian Alps

IRELAND

The Wild Atlantic Way and
   Western Ireland
Walking the Wicklow Way

ITALY

Alta Via 1 – Trekking in
  the Dolomites
Italy's Sibillini National Park
Shorter Walks in the Dolomites
Ski Touring and Snowshoeing in
  the Dolomites
The Way of St Francis
Trekking in the Apennines
Trekking in the Dolomites
Trekking the Giants' Trail: Alta Via 1
  through the Italian Pennine Alps
Via Ferratas of the Italian Dolomites
  Vols 1&2
Walking and Trekking in the
  Gran Paradiso
Walking in Abruzzo
Walking in Italy's Cinque Terre
Walking in Italy's Stelvio
  National Park
Walking in Sicily
Walking in the Dolomites
Walking in Tuscany
Walking in Umbria
Walking Lake Como and Maggiore
Walking Lake Garda and Iseo
Walking on the Amalfi Coast
Walking the Via Francigena
  pilgrim route – Parts 2&3
Walks and Treks in the
  Maritime Alps

MEDITERRANEAN

The High Mountains of Crete
Trekking in Greece
Treks and Climbs in Wadi Rum,
  Jordan
Walking and Trekking in Zagori
Walking and Trekking on Corfu
Walking in Cyprus
Walking on Malta
Walking on the Greek Islands –
  the Cyclades

NEW ZEALAND
AND AUSTRALIA

Hiking the Overland Track

NORTH AMERICA

The John Muir Trail
The Pacific Crest Trail

SOUTH AMERICA

Aconcagua and the Southern Andes
Hiking and Biking Peru's Inca Trails
Torres del Paine

SCANDINAVIA, ICELAND
AND GREENLAND

Hiking in Norway – South
Trekking in Greenland – The Arctic
  Circle Trail
Trekking the Kungsleden
Walking and Trekking in Iceland

SLOVENIA, CROATIA,
MONTENEGRO AND ALBANIA

Mountain Biking in Slovenia
The Islands of Croatia
The Julian Alps of Slovenia
The Mountains of Montenegro
The Peaks of the Balkans Trail
The Slovene Mountain Trail
Walking in Slovenia: The Karavanke
Walks and Treks in Croatia

SPAIN AND PORTUGAL

Camino de Santiago:
  Camino Frances
Coastal Walks in Andalucia
Cycling the Camino de Santiago
Cycling the Ruta Via de la Plata
Mountain Walking in Mallorca
Mountain Walking in
  Southern Catalunya
Portugal's Rota Vicentina
Spain's Sendero Historico: The GR1
The Andalucian Coast to Coast Walk
The Camino del Norte and
  Camino Primitivo
The Camino Ingles and Ruta do Mar
The Camino Portugues
The Mountains of Nerja
The Mountains of Ronda
  and Grazalema
The Sierras of Extremadura
Trekking in Mallorca
Trekking in the Canary Islands
Trekking the GR7 in Andalucia
Walking and Trekking in the
  Sierra Nevada
Walking in Andalucia
Walking in Menorca
Walking in Portugal
Walking in the Algarve
Walking on the Azores
Walking in the Cordillera Cantabrica
Walking on Gran Canaria
Walking on La Gomera and El Hierro
Walking on La Palma
Walking on Lanzarote
  and Fuerteventura
Walking on Madeira
Walking on Tenerife

Walking on the Costa Blanca
Walking the Camino dos Faros

SWITZERLAND

Switzerland's Jura Crest Trail
The Swiss Alpine Pass Route –
  Via Alpina Route 1
The Swiss Alps
Tour of the Jungfrau Region
Walking in the Bernese Oberland
Walking in the Engadine –
  Switzerland
Walking in the Valais
Walking in Zermatt and Saas-Fee

JAPAN AND ASIA

Hiking and Trekking in the Japan
  Alps and Mount Fuji
Japan's Kumano Kodo Pilgrimage
Trekking in Tajikistan

HIMALAYA

Annapurna
Everest: A Trekker's Guide
Trekking in the Himalaya
Trekking in Bhutan
Trekking in Ladakh

MOUNTAIN LITERATURE

8000 metres
A Walk in the Clouds
Abode of the Gods
Fifty Years of Adventure
The Pennine Way – the Path,
  the People, the Journey
Unjustifiable Risk?

TECHNIQUES

Fastpacking
Geocaching in the UK
Map and Compass
Outdoor Photography
Polar Exploration
The Mountain Hut Book

MINI GUIDES

Alpine Flowers
Navigation
Pocket First Aid and
  Wilderness Medicine
Snow

For full information on all our guides,
books and eBooks, visit our website:
www.cicerone.co.uk

CICERONE

Trust Cicerone to guide your next adventure,
wherever it may be around the world...

Discover guides for hiking, mountain walking, backpacking,
trekking, trail running, cycling and mountain biking, ski touring,
climbing and scrambling in Britain, Europe and worldwide.

Connect with Cicerone online and find inspiration.

- buy books and ebooks
- articles, advice and trip reports
- podcasts and live events
- GPX files and updates
- regular newsletter

cicerone.co.uk